■

AMERICA'S
ROLE
IN ASIA

■

ASIAN VIEWS

Tadashi Yamamoto

Pranee Thiparat

Abul Ahsan

2001

 The Asia Foundation

The Asia Foundation is a private, nonprofit, nongovernmental organization working to advance mutual interests in the United States and the Asia-Pacific region. It is funded by contributions from corporations, foundations, individuals, and governmental organizations in the U.S. and Asia; and an annual appropriation from the U.S. Congress. Through its programs, the Foundation builds leadership, improves policies, and strengthens institutions to foster greater openness and shared prosperity in the Asia-Pacific region.

AMERICA'S ROLE IN ASIA: ASIAN VIEWS

The Asia Foundation gratefully acknowledges The Henry Luce Foundation, the Japan Foundation Center for Global Partnership, and The General Electric Fund for their generous support of the America's Role in Asia project.

 THE ASIA FOUNDATION

465 California Street

14th Floor

San Francisco, CA U.S.A. 94104

www.asiafoundation.org

ISBN: 1-892325-03-9

Printed in U.S.A.

CONTENTS

CONTENTS

FOREWORD

In the past decade, a global cold war has ended and the world has entered into an era that is still undefined. In the absence of clear parameters to help us understand the post-Cold War world, the U.S. policy community is often inclined to look across the Atlantic. There, democratization has proceeded at a relatively brisk, if not unbroken, pace. Political and economic integration have begun to span and link both western and eastern Europe. The U.S. role in the Atlantic community— particularly in the strategic arena—is central and institutional, shaped by decades of methodical alliance-building.

A view across the Pacific is more complicated but no less important. Political systems in Asia are gradually becoming more open, some remarkably so, but the region is still host to the broadest spectrum of governments in the world. The Asian economic crisis of 1997-1998, from which Asian countries are gradually and sporadically recovering, affected not only U.S. economic and trade relations with the region, but also its political relations. Although the United States remains the hub and the guarantor of East and Southeast Asian security, threats in the region—especially along remaining Cold War fault lines in the Taiwan Straits and on the Korean peninsula— require the daily vigilance of U.S. and Asian policymakers. In South Asia, the entry of both India and Pakistan into the nuclear club opens a more lethal dimension to longstanding tensions over the status of Kashmir. In this increasingly complex and uncertain environment, it is even more important that American policy initiatives be crafted with central U.S. interests in mind, but reflecting in-depth understanding of Asian conditions and perspectives.

To aid policymakers in this task, The Asia Foundation launched the America's Role in Asia project in 1999. The occasion for the project's launch was the anticipation of a new administration and Congress in early 2001. However, we believe that the value of such an examination a decade after the Cold War's end is not dependent upon a single political event, however important the election of 2000 may be. In addition, we hope that the results of this project will also be of interest to Asian and American publics, whose involvement is integral to productive relations across the Pacific.

This project brought together outstanding policymakers, scholars, nongovernmental representatives, and businesspeople on each side of the Pacific to examine America's role in Asia, and challenges for U.S. policy in the regions of Northeast, Southeast, and South Asia. The American Task Force, chaired by Ezra Vogel of Harvard University and Casimir Yost of Georgetown University, met several times in the spring and summer of 2000 in Washington and in Cambridge, Massachusetts. Three groups of outstanding Asians, led by Mr. Tadashi Yamamoto of the Japan Center for International Exchange, Dr. Pranee Thiparat of the Institute for Security and International Studies at Chulalongkorn University, and Ambassador Abul Ahsan of the Independent University in Bangladesh, came together in Northeast, Southeast, and South Asian regional workshops in the spring of 2000. The American and Asian groups exchanged information on their meetings in order to keep one another informed of their deliberations. During this period, The Asia Foundation's field representatives also met to consider U.S. policy in Asia from their unique perspectives as country specialists and practitioners resident in Asia.

Informed by discussions of the American Task Force and the Asian regional workshop meetings, two reports have resulted from the project: *America's Role in Asia: American Views* and *America's Role in Asia: Asian Views*. Each offers recommendations for U.S. policy in the areas of security, economics, and politics. These documents drew heavily from the American and Asian meetings, but they are the responsibility of their respective authors. Ezra Vogel drafted the American report, and the three Asian chairs authored the Asian report. Comparisons between these two reports are both useful and inevitable. Nevertheless, we believe that each should stand on its own, in articulation of two sides of a relationship that is vital to the security and prosperity of Americans and Asians alike.

In February of this year, representatives of the American and Asian groups will meet at a conference in Seoul. This dialogue and debate will be a final, and crucial, phase of the America's Role in Asia project. Hosted by Han Sung-joo, former South Korean Foreign Minister and currently president of the Ilmin Institute for International Relations, the Seoul conference will also produce a brief report summarizing the points of commonality and divergence in U.S.-Asian relations. The Asia Foundation believes that such cross-fertilization, which has been the hallmark of the America's Role in Asia project, is an essential element for effective U.S. policy in Asia.

We are grateful to the five chairs for their hard work and their forbearance in this complicated but fascinating process, and to the American and Asian participants. As well, we thank The Henry Luce Foundation, the Japan Foundation Center for Global Partnership, and The General Electric Fund for their generous support of the America's Role in Asia project. Lastly, this project could not have been launched, much less successfully concluded, without the support of Asia Foundation staff in the Foundation's field offices in Asia, as well as its San Francisco and Washington offices.

William P. Fuller
President, The Asia Foundation

Catharin E. Dalpino
Project Director, America's Role in Asia Project

REGIONAL CHAIRS' PREFACE

The election of a new American president and a new Congress in 2000—the first of the new millennium—is an event of great importance not only to the United States but throughout the world, including the countries of Asia. As the world's lone superpower and one whose power and influence are deeply felt across the Pacific, the United States plays a crucial role in the security, economic, and political dynamics of Asia, a role unmatched by any other single power whether internal or external to the region.

At the same time, the countries of Asia continue on their own dynamic path of evolution and growth. Over the past 40 years, Asia has undergone a process of dramatic economic expansion, far-reaching political development, and rapid societal change that has transformed virtually every country in the region and thrust the region as a whole into a position of global importance and influence, even as the countries of Asia continue to wrestle with a number of complex internal and international challenges.

Certainly, the futures of Asia and the United States are by now inexorably linked, as developments in one part of the Asia-Pacific region tend to affect developments in other countries with increasing rapidity, regularity, and severity. In the new environment of globalization, no country can insulate itself completely from events elsewhere, although the exact nature and depth of interaction and engagement will of course vary for different countries at different times and under different circumstances. In this regard, the countries of Asia regard the United States as having legitimate interests in Asia, and as a country whose unprecedented military, economic, and political power—if handled wisely, consistently, and sensitively—can make an important, positive contribution to the future of the region. At the same time, Asia is also seeing the rise of a new confidence and assertiveness, and a corresponding desire to strengthen Asian regionalism, that will make the working out of positive relations with the United States a complex and ever-changing challenge for policymakers on both sides of the Pacific.

Within this evolving context of U.S.-Asian relations, The Asia Foundation's decision to launch a major project on America's Role in Asia to coincide with the election year in the United States is certainly timely. Every new U.S. administration and Congress faces its own unique set of challenges in developing its policy toward Asia, and the start of a new administration is always an appropriate time to review trends in the region, take stock of various policy options, and develop recommendations on a range of specific policy issues. In this regard, the formation under this project of a highly qualified, bipartisan American Task Force to analyze developments in the region, identify key American interests, and issue recommendations for the new administration and Congress is an initiative that should be welcomed.

At the same time, it is crucial, in our view, that in considering the future direction of U.S. policy in the region, Americans are also listening to Asian points of view and

seeking ways in which American interests and values
can be reconciled with those of its cross-Pacific neighbors in
order to advance the shared interests of both sides. For this
reason, the convening of a series of Asian regional workshops
under the America's Role in Asia project—in which experts
from Northeast Asia, Southeast Asia, and South Asia put
forward their own views, perspectives, and recommendations
for U.S. policy in Asia—represents a very positive and, indeed,
a crucial component of the project as a whole. In all, a total
of 42 participants representing 22 countries and regions
participated in the three workshops, held in Tokyo, Bangkok,
and Dhaka in the spring of 2000. The workshops provided
an opportunity for participants to analyze the key security,
economic, political, and social trends in their respective
regions, and to discuss the current and future U.S. policy
role in Asia. Following the three regional workshops, the
Chairs of the three workshops met in Tokyo to bring together
the results of the workshops and begin the process of writing
the regional reports and recommendations contained in
this volume.

Of course, given the vastness, diversity, and complexity
of Asia, no single project or publication can hope to capture
faithfully the full range of Asian views and perspectives on a
subject as complex and as nuanced as the U.S. role and U.S.
policy in Asia. Each subregion and, indeed, each country in
Asia is unique and is wrestling in its own way with its own set
of difficult security, economic, political, and social challenges,
all of which affect each subregion's and each country's relations
with the United States, and with one another. Rather than
approaching Asia as a whole, the America's Role project tried

to provide a more workable organizing framework for
U.S.-Asia relations by dividing Asia into the three subregions
of Northeast Asia, Southeast Asia, and South Asia, while
recognizing that even these distinctions are to a certain extent
arbitrary and limiting. This is especially true in the case of
Northeast Asia, where the development of subregional institutions at the intergovernmental level is not as advanced as
it is in South Asia and, especially, in Southeast Asia. Nor is it
the case that these subregions are developing in isolation from
one another. Events in the Taiwan Straits have ramifications
for Southeast Asia, South Asia's economic ties to Southeast
Asia are growing, India-Pakistan nuclear developments affect
China's security calculations, and so on.

In this volume of "America's Role in Asia: Asian Views,"
we have attempted to incorporate and synthesize the main
currents of analysis and perspective as expressed in the three
Asian subregional workshops on America's Role held earlier
this year. We have also offered a set of specific recommendations for U.S. policy with regard to each of the three subregions, as informed by the workshops. Finally, we have put
forward a series of policy recommendations for the United
States that are Asia-wide in scope, reflecting the main
common themes that emerged in the three subregional
workshops. While all the participants in the three workshops
made valuable contributions to the workshop discussions and
helped to inform our work, all of the reports and recommendations in this volume of "America's Role in Asia: Asian Views"
are solely the responsibility of ourselves as the workshop
Chairs and authors of the publication. We hope that this

volume makes a useful and positive contribution to the further understanding, and the future development, of U.S.-Asian relations.

Tadashi Yamamoto

Pranee Thiparat

Abul Ahsan

THE CHANGING CONTEXT OF U.S.-ASIAN RELATIONS

Asia is home to two-thirds of the world's population and is responsible for more than one-third of global economic output. It is a continent of remarkable diversity, with different histories, different cultural and religious traditions, different levels of economic development, and different political systems. Indeed, except for geographic proximity, it is impossible to link Asian nations into a coherent whole. Asia encompasses two of the world's three largest economies (Japan and China), some of the most technologically advanced societies on the planet (Japan, Korea, Taiwan, and Singapore), and a region well-endowed in natural resources (Southeast Asia). In stark contrast, Asia is also home to some of the world's poorest people (North Korea, Myanmar, and much of the Indian subcontinent).

Political development in Asia has been no less diverse. India is the world's largest democracy. Japan is Asia's most established liberal democracy. Since the end of the Cold War, many Asian nations have abandoned authoritarian forms of government and embarked on a path of democratic political development and reform, including South Korea, Thailand, Bangladesh, Cambodia, Mongolia, and, most recently, Indonesia. Their challenge now is to consolidate these new democracies through a complex process of institutional reform and enhanced state-society interaction, and to demonstrate to restive populations that democratic government can successfully deliver on the twin challenges of restoring economic growth and maintaining social stability. China, Vietnam, and Laos have pursued market economic reforms to various degrees, but have been steadfast in their resolve to maintain one-party rule. Both North Korea and Myanmar have pursued only minor economic openings to the outside world, while maintaining tight political controls over their populations.

> *Asia today contains three of the most complex, and potentially most threatening, security challenges anywhere in the world: cross-Straits tensions between China and Taiwan; the longstanding stalemate and potential military confrontation on the Korean peninsula; and the tense stand-off in Kashmir between the world's two newest nuclear powers, India and Pakistan.*

As in other regions, security concerns in Asia have traditionally centered on the nation-state, external threat perceptions, military balances, and other conventional defense issues. Indeed, Asia today contains three of the most complex, and potentially most threatening, security challenges anywhere in the world: cross-Straits tensions between China and Taiwan; the longstanding stalemate and potential military confrontation on the Korean peninsula; and the tense stand-off in Kashmir between the world's two newest nuclear powers,

India and Pakistan. The rise of China as a military power in the region, continuing uncertainty about Japan's security role, and the possible development and deployment of theater missile defense (TMD) and national missile defense (NMD) systems by the United States add important new elements to the overall security equation in Asia, all with ramifications for the major powers in the region and beyond. Certainly there is widespread agreement throughout the region that the successful management of relations among the United States, Japan, and China will be absolutely crucial to the future stability and prosperity of the region. But the evolving role of India within the South Asian context, and of an expanded Association of Southeast Asian Nations (ASEAN) that now encompasses all 10 countries of Southeast Asia, will be important as well.

As Asia wrestles with the "traditional" security challenges of China-Taiwan, India-Pakistan, and Korean peninsula relations, the region also faces a number of new security challenges at the subnational level, challenges closely linked to domestic economic and political issues in different countries but which have important ramifications beyond national borders. Such problems as widespread poverty, environmental degradation, trafficking of arms and drugs, ethnic and religious conflict, and failed systems of governance can have profound effects on the stability of countries in the region, especially given the processes of rapid economic and political change that almost every country in the region is now experiencing. Indeed, in much of Asia it is increasingly difficult to isolate security concerns from the economic and political realms, and vice versa. All are intertwined in a new regional and global dynamic

that makes traditional labels and categories increasingly problematic and limiting.

*Adding to the complexity of the post-Cold War
era is the rising importance of nonstate actors
in national and international affairs, a trend
that reflects the growing democratization
of the Asia-Pacific region and affects virtually
every country in the region, including, of
course, the United States.*

Adding to the complexity of the post-Cold War era is the
rising importance of nonstate actors in national and international affairs, a trend that reflects the growing democratization
of the Asia-Pacific region and affects virtually every country
in the region, including, of course, the United States. While
foreign policy was once the exclusive purvue of government
officials and a small group of foreign policy professionals, in
recent years we have seen a proliferation of new institutional
actors and interest groups—the business community, the
media, and civil society advocacy groups of all kinds—that have
their own views on foreign affairs issues and are increasingly
being heard. Importantly, these new nongovernmental actors
not only have increasing influence on the foreign policies of
their respective states; they also maintain links with counterparts in other countries and utilize these links to create
transborder coalitions on various issues (human rights, the

environment, rights and status of women, etc.) that generate their own influence in the international affairs arena. This trend toward the "pluralization" of foreign policy is likely to increase in the coming years with the rapid spread of information technology, adding further to both the complexity and the dynamism of international affairs in the region and around the world. Whether this trend results in greater instabilty in the management of international affairs, or instead represents a positive opportunity to mobilize new energies, new skills, and new resources to help solve complex global problems that governments alone are unable to solve, remains to be seen.

With the end of the Cold War, the idea of "globalization" has emerged as a defining concept for analyzing key international and domestic trends in the world. Certainly in the Asia-Pacific region, the rapidly increasingly flows of information, ideas, capital, goods, and people that we associate with the globalization process has had a profound effect on the development of the region, contributing to the highest economic growth rates in human history, lifting hundreds of million of people out of poverty, and creating a confidence, dynamism, and new assertiveness in the fast-growing countries of Asia that has important reverberations around the globe. Globalization has also had the effect of making people more aware of one another, and generating greater interdependence: increasingly, events and problems in one country or region can have important spill-over effects into other countries and regions as well.

In principle, such interdependence should lead to greater cooperation among nations, as there is a clear need for common approaches and cooperation in dealing with common challenges and successfully addressing the range of global problems that transcend national borders. But at the same time, we have seen that globalization can also, in many instances, generate a reaction of nationalistic or localized backlash against rapid societal change and the import of foreign ideologies and viewpoints associated with the globalization process. This desire to preserve and assert political, economic, and cultural autonomy against what are perceived as the universalizing trends of globalization is likely to be a key factor in U.S.-Asian relations in the coming decade, to the extent that globalization is closely associated with the political and economic power and the policy agenda of the United States. More broadly, globalization has created something of a paradox: on the one hand, the emergence of strong global forces pushing in the direction of greater interaction, internationalism, and common standards; on the other hand, the increasing identification with what are often subnational—and even local—political and cultural frames of reference. In this sense, the era of globablization in Asia, as elsewhere, is creating simultaneous pressures on the nation-state both from "above" (in the form of emerging universal norms and standards and international institutions) and from "below" (in the form of restive societies often divided along religious, ethnic, and regional lines and no longer willing to grant a monopoly of decisionmaking authority to government). Indeed, perhaps at no time have the pressures on government been greater, or the challenges more complex, than today. Ultimately, of course, all countries are forced to weigh the very real opportunities stemming from globalization against its potential downsides, and to make their policy decisions accordingly as best they can, while knowing that complete insulation is no longer an option, not even for North Korea.

Alongside the rise of globalization, and in fact closely intertwined with it, has been the emergence of the United States as the dominant power in the Asia-Pacific region, and in the world. With the decline of communism as both a political and economic system and as an ideological counterweight, democracy and the market economy are increasingly accepted as the desired norm throughout the world, including Asia. In this post-Cold War era, the United States, as the world's lone superpower, enjoys a level of military, economic, and political predominance around the world—and a resulting array of global interests and responsibilities—that is unprecedented in its history.

The Asian economic crisis that began in 1997 provided an additional boost to the perceived strength of the United States relative to other countries in the region. Not only did the U.S. remain virtually untouched by the economic contagion and slowdown that affected so profoundly its main trading partners in the region; the crisis also called into question some of the basic assumptions about the central role of the state and the strong business-government relationships that undergirded the success of the "East Asian growth state" as an alternative to the American model of economic management and development. American leadership in the field of information technology, with its emphasis on rapid innovation and flexibility, has further widened the economic gap in recent years, even as many of the affected economies in Asia have begun the return to positive growth and taken their own important steps to enter the "new economy."

Within the United States itself, of course, there is a great deal of uncertainty as to how American military, economic, and political strength should best translate into effective foreign policy, and ambivalence about the depth and breadth of America's engagement with the world, including Asia and the Pacific. As the world's only superpower, the United States has clear responsibilities for maintaining security and prosperity around the globe, yet the American people are traditionally inward-looking. Foreign policy is never high on the list of most Americans' priorities, and the U.S. is not always comfortable

A major challenge for the United States in Asia will be to consider (along with its allies and friends in the region) whether its existing framework of bilateral security alliances with key Asian states—especially Japan and Korea—will need to be adjusted or amended in response to a changing security environment in the region, including, perhaps, a process of reduced tension and gradual reconciliation on the Korean peninsula.

seeing its own interests and its own future as closely tied to, or dependent upon, the interests, actions, and decisions of others. In the coming years, a major challenge for the United States in Asia will be to consider (along with its allies and friends in the region) whether its existing framework of bilateral security alliances with key Asian states—especially Japan and Korea—

will need to be adjusted or amended in response to a changing security environment in the region, including, perhaps, a process of reduced tension and gradual reconciliation on the Korean peninsula. A related question for American foreign policy in Asia will be the extent to which the United States will be supportive of new multilateral approaches and institutions for dealing with complex security and economic issues in the region. Certainly, there is growing interest on the Asian side in the development and strengthening of such multilateral institutions (witness the growth of the ASEAN+3 process), some of which will not include the United States, just as there is concern that the United States sometimes chooses to act unilaterally rather than within the framework of accepted multilateral institutions such as the United Nations.

Taken as a whole, the countries of Asia welcome American engagement in the region, and are probably more concerned about potential American inattention than potential American dominance. Given the rapid pace of change in regional affairs and the uncertainties that characterize the region's security, economic, and political situation, the presence of the United States, including the security presence, as a relatively benign power is seen, on balance, as making a positive contribution to regional stability and security. The American appeals for democracy, good governance, and human rights find general, but certainly not universal, acceptance in Asia, while the U.S. market remains crucial to Asia's full economic recovery and future growth. The U.S. remains the destination of choice for Asia's best university students, and the cultural and "people-to-people" ties across the Pacific are extremely strong and continue to grow.

At the same time, there is a growing assertiveness in Asia that the United States needs to be mindful of, without overreacting to. As societies with thousands of years of rich history and cultural achievement, as nation-states that rose out of the legacy of colonialism and the destruction of the Second World War, as economies that have stunned the world with their record of achievement over the past four decades— the countries of Asia are seeking to define their own place in the world and to have a voice in shaping that world. While there are, of course, profound differences and disagreements among the different countries and subregions of Asia, there is also a growing interest in exploring the similarities and shared hopes that may form the basis for greater regional cooperation in the future. Such improved relations and expanded coopera- tion among the Asian nations themselves need not come at the expense of the United States, and could in fact help to advance American interests by contributing to greater stability and prosperity in the region. Nor does the development of a greater sense of "Asian" consciousness and identity need to preclude the emergence of an "Asia-Pacific community" of peoples and nations that brings Asia and the United States together in a common endeavor to shape a common future. To the extent that the United States serves as a constructive partner in building this Asia-Pacific community—consistently engaged but not domineering, maintaining strength but seeking mutual gain, and standing for its values but exhibiting patience and respect toward different views and approaches—it will find a welcoming response in the region.

NORTHEAST ASIA

OVERVIEW

The strategic significance of Northeast Asia continues to grow.
United States ties to Northeast Asian allies and friends span
the range of security, economics, culture, and politics. The
importance of longstanding U.S. alliances and security relationships in the region is further buttressed by the growing promi-
nence of Northeast Asia's economies, both as leading American
trading partners and important players in the global economy.
Japan and China are the world's second and third largest
economies, Japan is the world's largest bilateral aid donor,
and the region as a whole represents the globe's largest market.
Two of the region's major powers, Russia and China, are nuclear,
and China's influence in the world is likely to increase steadily
over the course of the 21st century. In this security context,
it is critically important that the Unites States and Japan
maintain their alliance relationship, even as the relationship
adjusts to reflect changing circumstances in the two countries,
and in the region. It is also crucial that the United States
develop a stable, constructive relationship with China, one that
encourages China's responsible role in contributing to regional
stability. Other overarching, long-term objectives in the region
include achieving peace and reconciliation on the Korean
peninsula, the easing of cross-Straits tensions between China

and Taiwan, and the incorporation of Russia into a peaceful and stable set of regional relationships. Security and stability in Northeast Asia are essential ingredients if the Asia-Pacific region as a whole is to flourish.

While there is a general recognition in Northeast Asia that continued American engagement, and the maintenance of a strong security presence in the region, remains crucial to the security and prosperity of the region, there is a perception that the U.S. sometimes pursues its foreign policy objectives in a heavy-handed manner. Most Northeast Asians support the values and principles that America espouses—open markets, free trade, democracy, human rights, the free flow of information, and an open society—but believe the U.S. must better understand the diversity and complexity of the region's political, economic, and social development. It is also widely felt that the U.S. needs to pursue its foreign policy objectives with greater consistency and sensitivity, and to approach regional issues within more of a multilateral framework of dialogue and cooperation, rather than unilaterally.

Though democracy and market liberalization are generally viewed positively in Northeast Asia, it is important that the United States not be seen as promoting its particular political and economic system as a model that is appropriate for all countries at all times. Rather, the U.S. needs to take into account that each country in the region is undergoing complex processes of political and economic change, in some cases exacerbated by the economic crisis, and that such processes can be difficult, uneven, and contentious. In this climate, the United States would do well to demonstrate more patience and a less doctrinaire approach to political and economic reform as different countries work their own way forward in reconciling emerging global pressures and standards with their own particular needs and circumstances. Finally, it is essential that dialogue and exchange at all levels be expanded among the countries of the region, including the United States, in order to create the mutual respect, understanding, and sense of shared interests and a shared future that will be essential to developing an Asia-Pacific community of nations in the 21st century.

SECURITY ISSUES

At the advent of the new millennium, the United States' preeminence in global affairs represents an important and defining factor in the security equation of Northeast Asia.

> *It is imperative that the United States manage its bilateral relations with both Japan and China effectively. This is a task of paramount importance for American diplomacy that will either positively or negatively affect the future of Northeast Asia and the entire Asia-Pacific region.*

Given its robust economy and military superiority, the U.S. is likely to retain its predominant position for another decade, if not longer. On the whole, the countries of Northeast Asia regard the American security presence as a welcome, even essential, force for peace and stability in the region. Yet no nation, even the strongest, can go it alone in an increasingly interdependent world. In this regard, the ability of the United States to work productively with other countries in the region through regular consultation and in the pursuit of shared interests will be critical to the region's future.

To create an overall security climate conducive to peace and stability in Northeast Asia, it is imperative that the United States manage its bilateral relations with both Japan and China effectively. This is a task of paramount importance for American diplomacy that will either positively or negatively affect the future of Northeast Asia and the entire Asia-Pacific region. The United States-Japan Security Treaty remains the cornerstone of both American and Japanese strategic policy in East Asia, and the alliance is generally viewed and accepted as a stabilizing force in the region. Though a majority of Japanese believe the two countries will continue to be good partners in the 21st century, a growing number of Japanese support greater Japanese independence and assertiveness in addressing their country's new defense challenges. This change in attitude may reflect, in part, a shift in power from the Japanese bureaucracy to political parties, the legislature, and civil society groups, to the point that security issues have now become part of the public policy debate in Japan. Given such sentiment, it would not be surprising if Japan were to begin to play a somewhat more independent role in international affairs, and to seek greater equality in its relations with the United States, while still retaining the strong bilateral partnership between the two countries.

The single biggest challenge facing the United States in Northeast Asia at the dawn of the 21st century is likely to be managing its difficult relationship with China. Simply put, the U.S. and China must find a way to cooperate with one another in order to ensure peace and stability in the region. China's views about the American leadership role in the region represent a combination of respect, suspicion, and unease. Though China respects the United States' economic strength and admires its ability as the world's innovator in high-technology, China also views the strong security role of the U.S. and the potential use of American military power in the region as reflecting an American desire to dominate the region and, through a policy of "containment," to prevent China from assuming its rightful role as an important regional power. This Chinese sentiment was exacerbated by the American bombing of the Chinese embassy in Belgrade. Though the U.S. has explained that this was an unfortunate accident, many in China viewed the bombing as an attempt to humiliate their

> *While future Chinese actions toward the U.S. may seek to avoid direct confrontation, the possibility of the two countries engaging in conflict over Taiwan cannot be ruled out.*

country in the eyes of the international community. With this ambivalent view of American power and intentions, it is difficult for China to accept fully the argument that a continued

U.S. forward-deployed military presence is necessary for the maintenance of peace and stability in the region.

Since the end of the Cold War, China's foreign and security policies have been heavily focused on Taiwan, and it tends to judge other countries largely based on their position on the Taiwan issue. In this regard, any support for Taiwan is construed in Beijing as a threat to China's sovereignty. It is clear that China will remain steadfast in its goal of reunifying Taiwan with the mainland. And, while future Chinese actions toward the U.S. may seek to avoid direct confrontation, the possibility of the two countries engaging in conflict over Taiwan cannot be ruled out. When China fired missiles into the seas around Taiwan's major ports in 1996, the U.S. demonstrated its commitment to the defense of Taiwan by sending two aircraft carriers into the Taiwan Straits. This was the most significant display of U.S. naval power in the region in decades. To avoid such occurrences in the future, Beijing, Taipei, and Washington will all need to handle the Taiwan issue with great care and restraint.

Though Taiwan's economic performance and successful multiparty political system are accomplishments in which its people can justifiably take great pride, the establishment of democracy in Taiwan has also tended to make cross-Straits relations more complex and uncertain by adding new actors and new policy voices into the equation. Certainly, China faces difficult choices in dealing with the Taiwan issue. A softened stance toward Taiwan could give the wrong signal that Beijing might tolerate Taiwan independence and would not take forceful action against it. On the other hand, a more aggressive posture could produce a marked deterioration in U.S.-China relations and result in increased support for Taiwan's independence both in Taiwan and in the United States. China's current policy seems to aim at persuading the U.S. to encourage Taiwan to act responsibly and not aggravate cross-Straits tensions through actions or statements that Beijing would regard as provocative. Given this climate, there is a strong view among all the countries in the region that China and Taiwan must both exercise restraint so as not to destabilize the entire region, and that the U.S. should encourage both parties to resume dialogue and make all efforts to avoid confrontation.

Against this backdrop of recurrent tensions between Beijing and Washington over Taiwan looms the issue of the

> *There is a widespread view in Northeast Asia that if the U.S. elects to develop theater missile defense and national missile defense systems, China, as well as other nations in the region, would feel compelled to increase its own military capabilities as a result. This would likely set off an arms race that would only serve as a detriment to long-term peace and security in the region.*

possible development and deployment of theater missile defense (TMD) and national missile defense (NMD) systems by the United States. For its part, China is concerned that if the U.S. were to incorporate Taiwan under a TMD defense umbrella, it would reduce Taiwan's vulnerability to potential military threat from China, which might in turn encourage greater independence sentiment among the Taiwan population. And while China may understand the logic of why the U.S. would want to develop TMD to protect America's 100,000 troops stationed in Japan and South Korea, or to develop NMD to reduce the threat from a "rogue state," it nonetheless tends to oppose both systems because they are viewed as hindering China's national defense capabilities and limiting its strategic options, and thus its strategic influence.

Other states in the region have also expressed concern about TMD and NMD. Indeed, there is a widespread view in Northeast Asia that if the U.S. elects to develop TMD and NMD systems, China, as well as other nations in the region, would feel compelled to increase its own military capabilities as a result. This would likely set off an arms race that would only serve as a detriment to long-term peace and security in the region. Further, many Northeast Asians believe that in embarking on the development of TMD and NMD capabilities, the United States is again demonstrating a "unilateralist" approach in pursuing its own objectives in the region without sufficient consultation with other key actors. They feel the U.S. needs to do a much better job of clarifying its rationale for developing TMD and NMD given the great skepticism in the region about the possible deployment of these systems. In this regard, conducting a comprehensive and balanced discussion with the key countries in the region on TMD and NMD would be a useful and welcome step for the next American administration to take.

While the countries of Northeast Asia generally would prefer the U.S. to pursue more of a multilateral approach to security issues in the region, by no means do they favor a U.S. withdrawal from the region, nor do they want China or any other country to gain preeminence in East Asia. Certainly, it is accepted that China has a legitimate role to play as a rising regional power. But it is hoped that China will play this role in a constructive and responsive manner, demonstrating moderation and consistency in its policies and operating within the framework of established norms and institutions. China's participation in regional fora, such as the Asia Pacific Economic Cooperation (APEC) forum and the ASEAN Regional Forum (ARF), as well as its cooperative role on the Korean peninsula, is seen by others in the region as positive steps as China assumes a larger role on the regional and global stage.

After 50 years of confrontation, the leaders of North and South Korea met for the first time in June 2000 in an effort to work toward peace and reconciliation on the divided peninsula and to begin the difficult process of reunification. While talks did not address contentious security issues such as North Korean missile and nuclear weapons development or the presence of 37,000 U.S. troops in South Korea, Northeast Asians hope that the North-South summit will usher in an era of increased cooperation and a reduction in tension on the volatile peninsula. Making the Korean peninsula peaceful and secure is a challenge for the entire region, and it is important that the U.S., Japan, and China, as well as Seoul and Pyongyang, are all involved in assisting the reconciliation process in constructive ways.

As a final component to the security equation in Northeast Asia, it will be important to integrate Russia into a constructive network of bilateral and multilateral relationships in the region, including efforts to expand economic cooperation between the Russian Far East and the countries of Northeast Asia. It is realistic to assume that over the next 10 to 20 years, Russia will begin to reassert itself in regional and global affairs, and efforts should be made now to ensure that this process develops in ways that safeguard regional stability through the establishment of cooperative relations with Russia's regional partners.

In overall terms, there are some important, positive signs for the future of security relations in Northeast Asia. Tensions between the two Koreas have been reduced, at least temporarily, and the U.S., South Korea, and Japan have increased their cooperation on North Korea. China and Japan have each improved their relations with South Korea significantly. Despite China's reservations, no country in Northeast Asia wants to see a U.S. withdrawal from the region. Such a withdrawal would create a power vacuum in Northeast Asia that would add an element of uncertainty and likely contribute to a less stable political and military environment as countries respond to these new uncertainties. On the other hand, the perception that the world has become "unipolar" given the U.S.' predominant military and economic strength creates its own set of challenges for the effective management of regional affairs. Certainly, there is a strong sentiment in the region that the United States could do a better job of consulting with others in the region on issues of common concern. Greater American receptiveness to the development and strengthening of multilateral institutions and approaches to dealing with complex regional issues would also be welcome, and would help to avert the criticism that the United States tends to act unilaterally or always within the framework of its established bilateral security arrangements. Over time, the broad acceptance of, and reliance upon, American leadership in the Asia-Pacific region will increasingly depend on the skills of American foreign policy in harmonizing the pursuit of its own national interests with the needs and interests of the region as a whole.

ECONOMIC ISSUES

The United States' economic importance to Northeast Asia, and vice versa, cannot be overstated. The United States, Japan, and China are the world's three largest economies and Japan, China, Taiwan, and South Korea represent four of the top 10 U.S. trading partners. The United States' long-standing role as the primary market for Asian exports has become even more important as Asian countries seek to recover from the economic crisis.

Because of the extensive economic interests the U.S. and Northeast Asia have with one another, economic and trade relations are inevitably complex and at times contentious. The U.S. has at times been very aggressive in its financial, trade, and business diplomacy on a bilateral basis, and its policy has not always been consistent, creating tensions with trading partners in the region. As in security matters, the United States' economic and trade policies have been pursued primarily on a bilateral basis, raising questions about the United States' commitment to multilateral economic cooperation.

On the whole, however, there is no question but that the United States is perceived as the crucial engine of growth for Asian economies and absolutely vital to the economic well-being of the entire region. Further, the United States is admired as a center of creativity and innovation and, in some respects, as a model for the development of new technologies and services that are likely to become even more important in the future. The Asian economic crisis and the dominance of American information technology firms have only added to the perception of American economic might relative to the countries of Asia, in marked contrast to the situation only a decade ago.

As Asia struggles to recover from the crisis, many Asians believe that the U.S. is justified in demanding that needed reforms be implemented in Asia—free trade, open markets,

> *There is also widespread feeling that the U.S. expects countries to change their policies and structures overnight and is insensitive to complex domestic factors and dynamics that each country in the region must wrestle with in carrying out reforms according to its own needs and desired pace of change.*

rule of law, transparency in financial institutions, greater accountability of government agencies, unimpeded access to information, etc. But there is also widespread feeling that the U.S. expects countries to change their policies and structures overnight and is insensitive to complex domestic factors and dynamics that each country in the region must wrestle with in carrying out reforms according to its own needs and desired pace of change. As a result, U.S. pressure to reform is often resisted and resented—whether it is U.S. criticism of Japan's efforts to revitalize its economy or China's reluctance to open its markets to foreign competition. Moreover, such pressure by the U.S. can serve to complicate or undermine the work of reform advocates inside those countries. In this climate, the U.S. might be more successful if it sought to advance mutual economic interests in the region through more of a multilateral approach. For example, instead of the U.S. seeking remedy for trade disputes through bilateral (really unilateral) mechanisms such as Super 301 legislation and anti-dumping tariffs, disputes would be better handled through multilateral bodies as the World Trade Organization (WTO).

In the longer term, it would be helpful for the U.S. to be more supportive of efforts to develop a framework of new regional institutions in East Asia—for example, the new ASEAN+3 initiative or an Asian Monetary Fund—even if such initiatives may not always include the United States. The U.S. should not fear such initiatives as long as they are in line to free-trade principles and are WTO compliant. Such regional institutions may also contribute to the emergence of shared practices and standards among economies in the region that will help to advance the very policy reforms that the United States now tries to encourage, not always successfully, through direct bilateral pressure.

Certainly, the Asian financial crisis brought home the power of globalization and a growing awareness that countries will increasingly have to respond to emerging global standards. But while many Northeast Asians recognize that their economies need to be restructured, they also tend to equate the concepts of "global standards" or "globalization" as synonymous with "American standards" or "Americanization." In this climate, many Northeast Asians fear that the rapid adoption of an American-style open economy and society would render them vulnerable to economic domination and undue cultural influence by the U.S. and other western nations. Moreover, as the pace of globalization has gained momentum, its true benefits and costs are not yet fully understood while its impact is quite uneven and, in some instances, has served to widen the disparity between the "haves" and "have-nots" both among and within individual countries. In sum, there are ambivalent feelings in Northeast Asia with regard to the promise—and the potential downsides—of globalization, which to a great extent mirror attitudes in the region toward the country that is most closely associated with the globalization phenomenon, the United States.

As Asian nations wrestle with the lessons of the economic crisis and the pressures and demands of globalization, there is a search underway among many Asian scholars and policy analysts for new approaches to economic and governance reform that will attempt to combine features of the American and East Asian models of economic development: a "third path" of development where Asian systems of governance and economic management can succeed in meeting global standards of performance and competitiveness while at the same time preserving some of their historical distinctiveness and cultural strength. In practice, this means that a new balance of power may be developing between the state and society, one in which power is gradually but steadily shifting from a highly centralized bureaucracy to a more diverse set of actors: elected politicians, civil society groups, and, of course, the market. How

> *The search for a new state-society relationship and for new developmental models is continuing in Asia and is something to which the U.S. must be sensitive.*

these various sectors will reconcile their competing interests through public policy debates and political institutions is not yet always clear. Nevertheless, the search for a new state-society relationship and for new developmental models is continuing in Asia and is something to which the U.S. must be sensitive. Freewheeling, American-style capitalism is not necessarily the end-product—and certainly not the goal— of most economic reform processes currently underway in Northeast Asia, just as the processes of political reform underway in the region may not be leading inexorably to American-style democracy.

In the foreign assistance area, while Japan has been in a decade-long recession, it has nonetheless spent far more than the United States to help other Asian countries recover from the 1997 economic crisis, and in its development cooperation programs more generally. Indeed, despite the economic progress many Asian nations have made since the end of the Cold War, humanitarian issues in Asia are still not being adequately addressed. Deeper disparities between "haves" and "have-nots" in the region do not serve the long-term interests

It is widely hoped in the region that the next U.S. administration will work with Japan and other countries in increasing the flow of bilateral and multilateral foreign assistance to help meet basic development challenges still facing many Asian countries.

of either the U.S. or Asian countries. In this regard, it is widely hoped in the region that the next U.S. administration will work with Japan and other countries in increasing the flow of bilateral and multilateral foreign assistance to help meet basic development challenges still facing many Asian countries. Given the growing importance of information technology to the international economy, it is hoped further that the U.S. will provide assistance to help less developed nations reduce the gap in this area.

As China continues its extraordinary economic growth over the next decade, its economic influence will surely continue to grow both regionally and globally. In this context, it is encouraging that, after years of contentious annual debate, the U.S. Congress has decided to grant normal trading status to China on a permanent basis, which should contribute to more productive and stable U.S.-China relations and also serve

to integrate China more fully into the international trade and
financial system. China's expected membership in the WTO
(to be followed almost certainly by Taiwan) will be important
for the region's economic development and will contribute to
China's own efforts to restructure its economy in ways that will
not only benefit China but also open up the Chinese market to
trade and investment from other countries.

POLITICAL AND SOCIAL ISSUES

As in other areas of policy, the primacy of American power
in the post-Cold War world has a tangible effect on political
and social relations of the Northeast Asian countries with the
United States. In addition, the rise of globalization, which some
regard as a direct consequence of U.S. power, has an impact
on Northeast Asian governments and societies, and complicates
U.S.-Asian relations. Although the U.S. economic and security
presence is still viewed by America's allies in the region as
beneficial and even essential, the broad spectrum of Northeast
Asian countries is increasingly uncomfortable with a United
States that thinks and acts unilaterally. In the social and political realms, this translates into a lack of adequate consultation
between Washington and the capitals of Northeast Asia on key
issues, and a more serious lack of knowledge about Asia in the
U.S. policy community and the American public on the whole.
These trends are worsening at a time when the United States
increasingly aims to influence the course of political change in
other countries toward democratization and the protection of
human rights, and the international community in general is
less reluctant to get "under the hood" of sovereign states.

Clearly, trends in Northeast Asia in the past decade are toward greater political openness. Political power is moving away from rigid bureaucratic control in Japan, South Korea, Mongolia, and Taiwan, where political parties are more central and civil society more assertive. Bureaucratic elites, who could safely assume a monopoly of power in the past, must now share power with elected leaders and nonstate actors. In turn, both elected and nonelected officials are increasingly called to account for their actions and the efficacy of their policies by citizen groups, and through administrative and legal reforms in the formal system. To be sure, rapid political change, even if it is beneficial, can create short and mid-term problems. The rise of parties has introduced coalition politics to systems— in Japan, South Korea, and Taiwan—that were previously attuned to one-party rule. If this has brought greater openness to policymaking at times, it has also occasionally brought incoherence. New governments are challenged to deliver eco- nomic and social progress when greater pluralism in the policy process and greater public pressure make it more difficult to govern. U.S. policy, which has encouraged broad democrati- zation in South Korea, Taiwan, and Mongolia over the past decade, should be readjusted and refined to reflect these new and more nuanced problems.

Since the end of the Cold War, the greatest attention to domestic political conditions in Northeast Asia by U.S. policymakers and the U.S. public has been focused on China. However, China's political path is by no means clear. The course of its domestic politics will affect China's ability to engage and become further integrated into the international community, as well as more fundamental questions of economic development and social and political stability. To date, U.S. policy toward Chinese political affairs has lacked perspective and nuance; on the official level at least, it has tended to be simplistic and ideological. Some advances in political liberalization, which encourage checks and balances at the local level, have been seen at the local level in China, but they do not at

> *If China moves toward a new political structure, it is not apparent that it will emulate the American model, even if the momentum is toward greater openness and reform.*

this time represent movement toward an American-style democracy. As economic reforms continue in China, and as the leadership considers the need for greater political reforms in response, the Chinese are studying several models of governance. If China moves toward a new political structure, it is not apparent that it will emulate the American model, even if the momentum is toward greater openness and reform.

Political trends in Asia have affected relationships between and among the nations of Northeast Asia. As South Korea has become more democratic, for example, its relations with Japan, an established democracy, have improved. In a similar vein, shared democratic experience has increased Japanese public sympathy for Taiwan.

However, democratization is seldom a straightforward process and some countries, particularly those such as

Russia and Mongolia which are experiencing severe economic hardship, could see reversals. Moreover, whether a country is moving briskly toward democratization or only beginning to experiment with political openness, it is clear that each will follow its own path. External pressure to change, whether from the United States or another Asian country, is likely to have far less influence than internal political and social dynamics.

Overall U.S. relations with the countries of Northeast Asia, where the United States has vital security interests and an extensive economic stake, are in need of improvement. The recent tendency in American foreign policy to compartmentalize issues, rather than to focus on the underlying long-term relationship, often makes U.S. policy less than the sum of its parts. Moreover, as U.S. policymaking becomes more pluralistic and more responsive to interest groups, it is often difficult for Northeast Asians to discern the direction or intention of U.S. relations with Asian countries. The fundamental structure of U.S. policy is not likely to change, but deliberate steps to improve communication between Washington and the Northeast Asian capitals are both possible and necessary. A related problem is the deficit in knowledge about Asia in the American policy community and the American public in general. As memories of American participation in the Asian "hot wars" (Korea, Vietnam) of the Cold War fade, concerted efforts are needed to educate Americans about the importance of the Northeast Asia region, and the views and concerns of Asian governments and societies.

REGIONAL RECOMMENDATIONS

1. In formulating and implementing policy on Northeast Asian security, the United States should utilize bilateral consultations more extensively and, where possible, take a multilateral approach.

Although there is widespread recognition of the leadership role played by the United States in Asian security, there is also increasing ambivalence—even among America's Asian allies—about the way in which the United States conducts its role as the primary power. Nations inevitably make bottom-line decisions about vital security issues based on their own national interests. To some extent, however, all of the nations of Northeast Asia have a common interest in regional stability and the reduction of tensions, whatever political differences they may have. As a source and guarantor of security in the Asia region, it benefits neither the United States nor the Asian nations for the U.S. to take a unilateral approach to these issues.

U.S. policymakers must make more deliberate and extensive efforts to consult Asian leaders on key security issues while they are in the process of formulating security policies. The most important example in this regard is the need for greater consultations on the development of an American national missile defense system, as well as a possible theater missile defense. Where multilateral consultations and actions are possible, such as on the Korean peninsula, the United States should support and advance such a framework. These multilateral arrangements are likely to be *ad hoc* for the foreseeable future, but may carry with them the seeds of a future regional security architecture.

---

2. The United States should help to secure peace and stability in the Taiwan Straits through efforts in preventive diplomacy, emphasizing to both China and Taiwan the need for responsible rhetoric and actions.

The cross-Straits issue is a vastly complicating one for U.S.-China relations. In the absence of formal alliances or unambiguous security mechanisms for the Taiwan Straits, the best avenue for U.S. influence is in diplomatic efforts with both China and Taiwan. These efforts should be even-handed and flexible. In the present cross-Straits climate, a formal role for the United States as a mediator is both improbable and inadvisable. Nevertheless, the U.S. should utilize its contacts with both China and Taiwan to encourage each side to view the other in a more balanced and fully dimensional way, and to counsel moderation on both sides.

---

3. The United States should acknowledge and support regional institution-building efforts in East Asia. It should encourage even those regional proposals that exclude a formal role for the United States, but that support shared goals of reducing tensions, promoting free trade, and adhering to the rule of law.

In the wake of the Asian financial crisis of 1997-1998, the need to examine and to strengthen regional frameworks has become more apparent. At the present time, the main focus is on financial architecture, at the global, regional, and subregional level. As countries recover from the crisis and as China approaches accession to the World Trade Organization, interest is strengthened in adherence to common trade regulations and in multilateral regimes. At the same time, these are acknowledged to be distant goals. Protectionism, different rates of economic growth and reform among trade partners, and legal systems that are ill-equipped to enforce global trade rules must be addressed, and remedied. This is complicated by some nationalist resentments over the role of the United States and the international financial institutions during the financial crisis. As a result of these factors, new regional and subregional groups and arrangements are being proposed in Asia, some of which exclude the United States and other Western economic powers.

The United States should take a four-pronged approach to these developments. First, it should continue to press Asian governments for financial and economic reforms which will benefit the cause of regional free trade, as well as individual countries. Second, the United States should employ and demonstrate patience and a more long-term approach with Asian trading partners. Removing many of the barriers to free trade in Asian countries will require considerable domestic adjustment. Third, where possible the United States should work toward multilateral financial regimes, even if it means scaling back bilateral trade efforts and forfeiting some of the short-term gains to be had from bilateral pressure. Lastly, the United States should acknowledge and support regional and subregional groupings which advance the cause of free trade in Asia, whether or not they offer a formal role for the United States.

---

4. The United States should downplay pressure for Northeast Asian countries to build Western-style democracies and emphasize the need for governments to be more responsive and accountable.

The demand for good governance is growing in Northeast Asian countries that are still under some form of authoritarian rule, as well as those that are presently democratizing. Abandoning a high-profile democracy promotion effort in favor of encouraging more transparent and accountable government will enable the United States to promote greater openness in a range of Northeast Asian states, rather than only those that have made a formal commitment to democracy. Moreover, this approach is more appropriate for an outside actor (and more acceptable to most Asians), since it does not advocate or prescribe an exact form of government.

---

5. The United States should recognize the rise and development of civil society organizations in Northeast Asia, including in China, and strengthen linkages between U.S. civil society organizations and their Asian counterparts.

Just as policymaking in the United States has become more open to citizens' concerns, so is Asian governance and policymaking becoming more pluralistic. During the Cold War, American policymakers needed only to interact with their counterparts in Asian governments. In order to understand Asian concerns and craft more effective policies, U.S. policymakers must now take into account the views of a broader spectrum of Asian actors. Beyond official policymaking, U.S.-Asian relations will benefit from increased contact between Asian nongovernmental organizations (NGOs) and their American counterparts, particularly on issues of common concern (public health, education, environmental pollution). These linkages can be nurtured in a number of ways, ranging from assistance for programs that link NGOs across the Pacific, to the addition of an NGO dimension to official dialogues. The successful cooperation of American and Japanese NGOs through the U.S.-Japan Common Agenda is one example of such linkage.

---

6. The United States should initiate broad-based dialogues with Northeast Asian countries on a range of issues to promote ongoing discussion of a "Pacific Vision."

Modeled after the U.S.-Japan Common Agenda, these dialogues should identify issues of common interest and concern beyond the parameters of traditional policy. These issue areas might include the environment, human rights, care of aging populations, and the gap between "haves" and "have-nots." Dialogues should be based in societal as well as governmental relations, and include representatives from executive branches, legislatures, the media, business sectors, civil society groups, and academia. These networks will enable Northeast Asians and Americans to identify shared interests, explore differences of opinion in a constructive manner, and improve each side's understanding of the other's political and social dynamics.

---

7. American universities should be encouraged to strengthen Asian studies programs, to provide a broader base of educators in Asian affairs.

Increasing and maintaining American interest in Asian affairs, which is crucial to formulating policies that effectively promote U.S. interests in Northeast Asia, must go beyond dialogues and be rooted in the American education system. Programs in Asian studies should be strengthened, and more Americans should be encouraged to study in Asia. There is currently a serious imbalance in this regard. For example, presently only 1,400 American students attend Japanese educational institutions, while 40,000 Japanese students are enrolled in American colleges and universities. Long-term beneficial relations between the United States and the countries of Northeast Asia will depend on the existence of communities of policymakers, scholars, and everyday citizens who are knowledgeable about the history, culture, structures, and views of their partners across the Pacific.

SOUTHEAST ASIA

OVERVIEW

The forces of globalization—including trends toward democratization, free trade, market economies, and increasingly open societies—are driving fundamental political, economic, and social changes in the world as well as in the region. In this content, it is inevitable that the United States, as the foremost global power, and one whose power is closely associated with these global trends, is seen as having an important role to play in Southeast Asia's security, economic growth, and political and social development. Specifically, it is hoped that the United States can make a positive contribution to regional stability and security, maintain an open U.S. market for Asian exports, promote regional economic cooperation for broad-based growth, encourage good governance practices in appropriate ways, and assist the region in dealing with new global challenges such as environmental degradation, terrorism, and transnational crime. Southeast Asia wants to see balanced and stable relations among China, Japan, and the United States, without any one country dominating the region. There is concern that if this balance should be threatened, Southeast Asia will become polarized as it was during the Cold War, something none of the member ASEAN countries views as in its best interests.

Given that broad development trends in the region are generally moving in a direction that is in line with American interests, Southeast Asia believes that the U.S. must exercise more patience, restraint, understanding, and respect in its relations with the countries in the region. While American engagement is desired, Southeast Asian states are concerned that engagement should not become interference. Humanitarian intervention, as in the case of Kosovo, for example, can be troubling because of firmly held beliefs in the principles of national sovereignty and territorial integrity in Southeast Asia, while U.S. policies to promote democracy and human rights by linking them to trade issues are viewed as counterproductive. Moreover, America's dominance in a unipolar world and its critical role in Southeast Asia can sometimes lead to anti-American rhetoric in the region. It is important for U.S. and Southeast Asian policymakers to separate the rhetoric from the substance of relations, in order to advance mutual interests in a consistent and constructive way.

Southeast Asian states are concerned that there seems to be a lack of a long-term U.S. strategy toward the region, which may encourage other regional actors to exercise more influence. Southeast Asians do not wish their region to be viewed as an appendage of East Asia, but understood in its own terms as a region with its own history, its own dynamics, and its own aspirations and interests as it wrestles to meet the challenges of the future. For the foreseeable future, ASEAN will continue to be the only dominant organization in the region, but one that will need to increase its own internal cohesion and effectiveness in order for Southeast Asia to have a stronger voice in Asia-Pacific and global affairs.

SECURITY ISSUES

The economic crisis that swept Southeast Asia in 1997 has had
ramifications for the region far beyond the economic sphere.
A growing sense of uncertainty has replaced the optimism of
earlier years that Southeast Asia would see the emergence
of a more predictable and prosperous regional order with the
end of the Cold War. As the full effects of the economic crisis
have become clear, it has underscored the fact that many of
Southeast Asia's security problems in fact stem from domestic
issues—from political instability in Southeast Asia's largest
country, Indonesia, to persistent high levels of poverty in
ASEAN's new members. The region's inability to formulate
an effective response to the economic crisis has also raised
questions about the role and effectiveness of ASEAN itself as
a regional institution capable of responding to new, complex
challenges in the region. For the countries of Southeast Asia

> *In general, Southeast Asians believe that the
> United States does not pay enough attention
> to the region, often referring to American
> policy toward Southeast Asia as one of "benign
> neglect" or "indifference."*

to be successful in an increasingly competitive world, they
must work together, through ASEAN, to strengthen their
bonds of regional cooperation in order to contribute positively

to peace and prosperity in the region and the world. This strengthening of regional cooperation and "resilience" will also have the effect of attracting increased, more positive American engagement in the region.

In general, Southeast Asians believe that the United States does not pay enough attention to the region, often referring to American policy toward Southeast Asia as one of "benign neglect" or "indifference." For a majority of the Southeast Asian countries, the U.S.' security role and presence in East Asia is viewed as providing a crucial strategic balance for regional stability. The U.S. military presence is seen as vital to the overall security equation in Southeast Asia, and there is concern that the United States' apparent lack of a long-term strategy toward Southeast Asia and a possible reduction of the American security presence in the region might lead other regional actors to push for greater influence.

In this regard, China's role in the region inevitably receives a great deal of attention, both positive and negative. During the economic crisis, for example, China's pledge not to devalue its currency, even though it may have been in China's own interest to maintain its exchange rate, generated much goodwill in the region, especially when contrasted to the inaction on the part of the United States. In this instance, many Southeast Asians felt that the U.S. had disappointed its friends in the region while allowing China an opportunity to enhance its own reputation in Southeast Asia.

On broad security issues, however, China occupies an ambivalent position in the views of many Southeast Asians, as the country has territorial disputes with Vietnam, the Philippines, Malaysia, and Indonesia. In this context, a forward-deployed U.S. military presence in East Asia (troops in Korea and Japan and the U.S. Seventh Fleet) is widely seen as providing an important safeguard for regional stability,

> *Good relations between the U.S. and China are critical if Southeast Asia is to be peaceful and prosperous; it is in everyone's interests to have a China that is open and cooperative within a market-oriented economic system.*

especially given the difficulty of coordinating a unified response from ASEAN on issues related to the South China Sea. Nevertheless, Southeast Asian countries will continue to cultivate positive relations with China—and to limit their relations with Taiwan—in order to help ensure that China will act as a responsible regional partner. Indeed, it is widely felt in Southeast Asia that good relations between the U.S. and China are critical if Southeast Asia is to be peaceful and prosperous; it is in everyone's interests to have a China that is open and cooperative within a market-oriented economic system. At the same time, Southeast Asians emphasize that U.S. policymakers need to move beyond their tendency to focus overwhelmingly on China and Japan, to the extent that Southeast Asia becomes "merely an appendage of East Asia."

Although Japan looms large in Southeast Asia in terms of aid, trade, and investment, Southeast Asians voice concern over Japan's seeming hesitance about its security role and foreign policy in the region. This stands in marked contrast to what is seen as China's increasing assertiveness in regional and international security issues. At this juncture, the defining framework for Japan's involvement in the region continues to be limited to the U.S.-Japan security alliance. And even beyond security matters, for many Southeast Asians, Japan no longer exhibits the leadership potential that it once embodied in the 1980s during a period of extraordinarily dynamic economic growth. At the end of the 20th century, Japan seems mired in stagnancy, still a formidable economic force in the region but unable to generate and sustain critical domestic reforms and limited in its appeal and influence internationally.

Security concerns in the region, therefore, tend to focus on the U.S., China, and ASEAN, with Southeast Asians emphasizing the need to strengthen regional and multilateral institutions and approaches in responding to any number of regional concerns. Southeast Asian leaders are sometimes frustrated that despite the fact that ASEAN has been in existence for three decades, the U.S. continues to interact with ASEAN primarily on bilateral terms rather than in the aggregate. Many Southeast Asians also recognize, however, that ASEAN itself has never made a concerted effort to develop a sophisticated and comprehensive strategy of its own to deal with the United States. Moreover, disparate responses from the individual ASEAN countries makes it very difficult for the U.S. to develop a consistent approach to the grouping as a whole. One important ASEAN initiative in this regard, the ASEAN Regional Forum (ARF), has succeeded in broadening official dialogue on security issues in the region and has been accepted and institutionalized as a viable, ongoing dialogue forum that has now expanded to include North Korea. However, given the complex multicountry territorial disputes in the South China Sea and ARF's inability to formulate a constructive response to the crisis in East Timor in 1999, many in Southeast Asia not only see a need to strengthen existing multilateral institutions, but are also increasingly open to considering the development of new multilateral structures for dealing with security challenges and crisis situations in

> *Efforts by the U.S. to cooperate on security issues within more of a multilateral framework would be welcomed in the region; this may be especially true in light of the American military intervention in Kosovo.*

the future. For such multilateral initiatives to be successful, American support will be essential.

In general, efforts by the U.S. to cooperate on security issues within more of a multilateral framework would be welcomed in the region; this may be especially true in light of the American military intervention in Kosovo. The position taken in Kosovo by the U.S. and its NATO allies—that the protection of human rights can take precedence over the principles of sovereignty and noninterference in a country's internal affairs—is troubling to many who live in a region deeply affected by social instability, ethnic conflicts, and religious tensions. While many Southeast Asians were horrified by the human rights atrocities taking place in Kosovo, most participants felt that it would have been more appropriate for the U.S. to seek a solution to the problem within the framework of the United Nations. Although such an unilateral military approach by the United States and NATO might be attractive in the short term, a U.S. failure to understand the depth of Southeast Asian concerns about national unity and the territorial integrity of sovereign states is likely to be detrimental in the long term. Certainly, given separatist sentiments in Aceh and Irian Jaya, and religious and ethnic conflicts in the Moluccas, national unity is at the top of the national agenda in Indonesia. National unity is also of significant concern in the Philippines and Myanmar. While the U.S. is on record as saying it supports Indonesia's territorial integrity and national unity, it would be helpful if the next U.S. administration were to state explicitly that it respects the territorial integrity and national unity of all of Southeast Asia, especially in light of uncertainties raised by the recent international interventions in Kosovo and East Timor.

Southeast Asians recognize that ASEAN faces significant challenges in the new global environment. Increasingly, domestic problems with significant impact on regional stability are pushing some in ASEAN to question the organization's adherence to a strict interpretation of the principle of non-interference. Environmental issues, the arms and drug trade, religious and ethnic conflicts, and the trafficking of women and children—these "new" security issues may require more cooperative efforts from ASEAN members than in the past. Moreover, although an inter-governmental form of cooperation remains central to ASEAN, the region's increasingly more open societies are giving nonstate actors such as nongovernmental organizations a stronger advocacy role on a wide range of issues concerning the environment and political, economic, and social change. Human rights NGOs in Thailand and the Philippines, for example, are increasingly outspoken in their criticism of Myanmar.

In this changing climate, there is likely to be increasing pressure on ASEAN itself to change in order to maintain its relevance and its leadership role for the future. And while ASEAN countries realize fully the need to achieve better cohesion in order to be effective, the challenge of building cooperation, solidarity, and consensus within the organization has been made more difficult by the expansion of ASEAN to include all 10 countries of Southeast Asia. While a 10-country ASEAN represents the fulfillment of a longstanding dream for organizational unity in Southeast Asia, the different political and economic systems of the new members (Vietnam in 1995, Laos and Myanmar in 1997, Cambodia in 1999) and their generally lower levels of economic development make the challenges of consensus-building within ASEAN a formidable one.

The addition of Myanmar has been particularly problematic, as the United States and Europe have maintained a policy of economic sanctions and isolation toward that country despite its entry into ASEAN. In truth, many Southeast Asians are also troubled by the human rights record and political intransigence of the leadership in Myanmar, and some still express disagreement with the decision to admit Myanmar as a member of ASEAN. Nevertheless, most Southeast Asians generally agree that the current ASEAN strategy of "constructive engagement" toward Myanmar, is the best policy option available and believe that the U.S.' policy of economic sanctions and isolation has not been helpful in improving human rights in Myanmar, nor has it helped to break the political impasse between the military and political opposition in that country. And while ASEAN is not in a position to bring about a process of domestic political reform in Myanmar, at the very least ASEAN can maintain lines of communication with the leadership in Myanmar to ensure that they understand regional and international concerns.

Finally, in an era of increased globalization and given the historically porous boundaries in parts of Southeast Asia, there is concern in Southeast Asia about the rise of transnational crime, most notably the trafficking of narcotics and individuals (particularly women and children), and the selling of small arms. In this regard, ASEAN has recently established a Center for Transnational Crime in Singapore, and would welcome American support and assistance in its anti-crime initiatives.

ECONOMIC ISSUES

Throughout most of the 1990s, economic growth rates in Southeast Asia were among the highest in the world, which was largely attributed to successful export-oriented trade policies. All Southeast Asian nations view the U.S. market as critically important: the U.S. is the first or second largest trading partner of almost every country in Southeast Asia and accepts some 21 percent of all of ASEAN's exports. While Americans have been buying Thai silk and sneakers made in Indonesia, they have also been buying value-added commodities such as computers, telecommunications hardware, and other electronic products. Since the advent of the financial crisis in July 1997, much of Southeast Asia's recovery and growth has been contingent on the robustness of the U.S. economy and its ability to consume imports from Southeast Asia. Should the U.S. economy stumble or protectionist sentiments in the United States rise, Southeast Asian economies could be greatly affected and trade liberalization efforts by ASEAN, the Asia Pacific Economic Cooperation forum, and the World Trade Organization would be hampered.

If the region is to regain its economic vitality and prosperity for the long term, however, many Southeast Asians believe that the region must go beyond its reliance on the U.S. market. There must be a greater willingness by other countries, particularly Japan, to open their markets, and serve as engines of growth for the region. At the same time, there is wide recognition in the region that, in this era of globalization, the ASEAN countries themselves must take steps to make their own economies more competitive. Although exports from Southeast Asia to the U.S. have risen 14 percent in the first six months of 2000, market share is being lost as exports to the United States from China and Mexico are rising rapidly. At the same time, U.S. foreign investment in ASEAN nations has been shifting to other developing countries. Low levels of investment continue to thwart recovery in the banking and financial sectors of many ASEAN countries, particularly Indonesia, Thailand, and the Philippines. Before Southeast Asia can begin to return to sustainable economic growth, enormous private and government debt must be reduced. Failure to do so could have serious repercussions for economic recovery and long-term development in Southeast Asia. Understanding and adopting best practices and standards in corporate governance will also be needed if ASEAN is to effectively compete in the global economy. As Southeast Asia has begun to recover from the economic crisis, some are concerned that complacency may be setting in and the pace of economic reform and banking restructuring slowing down. In this situation, there may be a useful role for the U.S. to play in providing technical assistance and access to models and best practices, whether in the region or internationally, on various issues of institutional reform and corporate restructuring. For example, it might be beneficial for both the U.S. and ASEAN if the U.S. provided increased

> *The U.S. needs to allow time for countries*
> *to liberalize their economies and should*
> *not be impatient or heavy-handed in insisting*
> *on across-the-board liberalization overnight.*

training opportunities for ASEAN officials in such areas as commercial law, banking, regulatory operations, accounting, and corporate governance.

While there is recognition in ASEAN that the U.S. could play a useful role in Southeast Asia's economic recovery through support for needed policy reforms, there is also a strong view that the U.S. needs to allow time for countries to liberalize their economies and should not be impatient or heavy-handed in insisting on across-the-board liberalization overnight. The modernization of Asia's economic and financial institutions, both public and private, is a work in progress that will take many years to accomplish. At a time when many ASEAN countries are pursuing significant economic reforms, these same countries are also grappling with political reforms that may go against powerful vested interests. In an era when countries around the world, including Southeast Asia, are wrestling to meet the challenges of rapid economic change and emerging global standards, the U.S. should be more patient and less arrogant in its approach. While U.S. assistance is needed, and indeed welcomed, it is not helpful when the U.S. engages in public criticism of other countries' political and economic systems, or crosses the threshold from engagement to interference.

Many Southeast Asians emphasize that while the region is appreciative of U.S. support and its leadership role, what also matters greatly is how that support is being offered. The

> *The way the message is delivered* matters *in Southeast Asia, and too heavy a hand in pushing for reforms can create a domestic political backlash that has the effect of making the task of reformers in Southeast Asia more difficult.*

countries in the region are independent states that see themselves as generally friendly toward the United States but are sometimes taken aback by the domineering approach of its official representations. More specifically, the United States may favor a set of policy prescriptions with regard to open markets and trading regimes with which Southeast Asian states are often in agreement; but the aggressive way in which these policy prescriptions are pursued can generate unnecessary resistance from countries in the region. In sum, the way the message is delivered *matters* in Southeast Asia, and too heavy a hand in pushing for reforms can create a domestic political backlash that has the effect of making the task of reformers in Southeast Asia more difficult.

One way the U.S. might effectively work with ASEAN in helping to achieve important financial and banking reforms in the region is through APEC. Many in Southeast Asia see the global financial architecture as being in some ways unfair to Asia since it is perceived that the World Bank and the International Monetary Fund (IMF) are weighted in favor of the U.S. and Europe, respectively. As such, APEC may provide a useful forum for the discussion and pursuit of financial and banking reforms that are important to Southeast Asia's future economic development.

By the same token, many Southeast Asians feel that the United States should be open to the development of new regional economic initiatives that may not include the United States, such as the idea for an Asian Monetary Fund and the development of the ASEAN+3 dialogue that brings together the 10 ASEAN countries along with Japan, China, and South Korea. Japan initially raised the concept of an Asian Monetary Fund during the Asian financial crisis in 1997, but the concept was soundly rejected by the U.S. out of fear that an Asian Monetary Fund would undermine the IMF and thus weaken the impetus for enacting strict austerity measures and structural reforms. Despite the U.S.' opposition, the idea of an Asian Monetary Fund has been resurrected and is gaining broader acceptance in Asia. The purpose of an Asian Monetary Fund would not be to replace the IMF, its supporters note, but to have a parallel and complementary structure in place that can help foster regional economic cooperation. An Asian Monetary Fund could also serve as an additional resource for countries in crisis. However, it is recognized that for an Asian Monetary Fund to be successful, it must adhere to established principles of transparency, accountability, and fairness and be generally in line with globally approved principles and standards.

Similarly, in Southeast Asian eyes, the U.S. should view more positively the regular meetings of ASEAN members with their regional partners in East Asia. ASEAN states created the ASEAN+3 initiative in order to expand foreign direct investment and trade, as well as to maintain a direct line of communication with Beijing, Tokyo, and Seoul. It should not be viewed as being directed against, or operating against the interests of, the United States. Nor should the U.S. raise objections to regional economic linkages under ASEAN+3 as long as these are WTO compliant.

Southeast Asians are hopeful that the U.S. will push for a new round of trade talks in the WTO, but they do not want to see a politicization of trade and economic issues. In the Southeast Asian view, the U.S. should clearly and consistently decouple trade issues from concerns over human rights. This is not to say that the U.S. should not be concerned with the protection of human rights; many Southeast Asians are also deeply concerned about human rights violations in the region. But the U.S. needs to be sensitive to the fact that a policy of linking the two issues, and doing so in a public manner, can end up doing more harm than good to the causes of both trade liberalization and democratic change. In this context, ASEAN is very pleased by the U.S. Congress' decision earlier this year to grant China permanent normal trade relations (PNTR), as it will ultimately permit the U.S. and ASEAN greater access to China's market through trade and investment, which will also assist China's integration into the international trading system.

Whereas the original members of ASEAN experienced almost a quarter century of solid economic growth prior to the economic crisis, its newest members (Vietnam, Laos, Cambodia, and Myanmar) remain some of the poorest countries in the world outside of sub-Saharan Africa. In fact, all of Southeast Asia still has tremendous developmental and human resource needs that must be addressed if the region is to successfully meet the challenges of the future. In this regard, the precipitous decline in U.S. foreign assistance over the past two decades is very much regretted by all the countries in Southeast Asia and particularly by those newer members of ASEAN that could most benefit from foreign aid. The decline in U.S. foreign assistance represents a missed opportunity for the U.S. to generate goodwill in the region and to assist processes of development and reform in Southeast Asia that would benefit all concerned. At the same time, the newer, less-developed countries of ASEAN are also critical of their more-developed colleagues on the foreign assistance issue, as development cooperation within the region, particularly with regard to technical assistance and training opportunities, has not been as forthcoming as had been hoped, at least in part because of the financial crisis.

In the past, many of Southeast Asia's current leaders benefitted directly from U.S.-funded educational and exchange opportunities which also served long-term U.S. interests. Although Japan has not become the engine of growth to help Asia escape its economic doldrums, it has nonetheless developed a strong reservoir of goodwill in Southeast Asia through its foreign assistance programs, which have become the largest in the world as those of the United States have declined. The next American administration, therefore, could make an important contribution to the mutual interests of Southeast Asia and the United States by greatly expanding its support for education and training programs for Southeast Asians in such areas as information technology, the environment, health, and agricultural development. Southeast Asia's ability to compete effectively in the global marketplace and move up the value-added manufacturing chain will help to ensure the region's prosperity and continued movement toward trade liberalization and political openness. American assistance in building the institutional and human resources capacity in the region to facilitate this process would be a worthwhile investment in the region's future.

POLITICAL AND SOCIAL ISSUES

In most of Southeast Asia, the basic principles of democracy, good governance, the rule of law, and human rights are increasingly accepted as both universal and positive. However, Washington's tendency to emphasize democracy and human rights in its foreign policy dealings with Southeast Asia is often viewed in the region as heavy-handed and insensitive to the nuances of each country's unique history, cultural background, and economic conditions.

In broad terms, there is no doubt but that the Southeast Asia region as a whole is much more democratic than it was 15 years ago, with democratic transitions having been successfully institutionalized in the Philippines and Thailand, and a difficult transition process now underway in Southeast Asia's largest country, Indonesia. In addition, in virtually every country in the region there is increased attention to issues of political reform and strengthening civil society and the rule of law. In this changing regional climate, where reforms are underway but where nationalist sentiments remain strong and respect for sovereignty and noninterference in the domestic affairs of others remain core principles of foreign policy, many in Southeast Asia argue that the United States would be more successful in advancing its democracy and human rights agenda abroad if it did so from the standpoint of facilitation and assistance, rather than through public criticism and pressure. Indeed, many in Southeast Asia make an explicit distinction between foreign assistance in supporting democratization efforts, which is welcomed if requested by local institutions and administered in ways that are respectful of state sovereignty, and foreign pressure for democratization, which is almost always resisted.

Southeast Asians also tend to view democratization and political reform as a long-term process, one whose directions, pace, and form must be determined by each country itself, based on its own history, culture, and the developmental needs of its own people. Greater American patience and appreciation of the complexities of these issues would find a welcome response in Southeast Asia.

On the whole, there is a strong sense in ASEAN that it wants (and needs) to become stronger, more unified, and more self-reliant. In this regard, the United States' dominance in a unipolar world and its important economic, political, and security role in the region can inevitably lead to a certain amount of nationalist backlash and anti-American rhetoric. It is important, therefore, that American and Southeast Asian policymakers make a special effort to separate the rhetoric from the substance of relations, be they bilateral or multilateral. Failure to do so would be counterproductive for both sides. Countries can also seek areas of cooperation with one another, even if not every aspect of their relations is smooth at a given time. Strong criticism of the U.S. on political issues among leadership circles in Malaysia, for example, has not prevented the country from maintaining mutually beneficial defense and economic relationships with the United States.

The search for regional solidarity and more multilateral approaches in Southeast Asia is a "natural" development, and one that the United States should support.

In general, it would do well if the U.S. recognizes that since it stands as the world's sole superpower, the asymmetry of power between the U.S. and Southeast Asia has understandably heightened the regional desire to strengthen multilateral institutions in order for ASEAN to have a greater voice in the global community. The building of regional institutions in Asia is not driven fundamentally by anti-Americanism but by a desire of people in the region to create institutions that reflect their own interests and serve their own needs. As such, the search for regional solidarity and more multilateral approaches in Southeast Asia is a "natural" development, and one that the United States should support.

Finally, many intellectual leaders in Southeast Asia, including those favorably disposed toward the United States, are concerned about the perceived decline of Southeast Asian studies in the U.S. in recent years, as the first generation of American specialists on Southeast Asia are beginning to retire and are not being replaced at the same rate. Without a sustained effort to maintain strong Southeast Asian studies programs in the U.S., American policymakers and the public alike will over time be much less well-informed about the region, with negative consequences for U.S.-Southeast Asian relations in the future. At the same time, Southeast Asians themselves must do a better job of informing themselves about the United States in all its complexities, including American society and values, the role of the U.S. Congress, and the pluralistic nature of American foreign policymaking in general. In other words, it is the responsibility of leaders on both sides of the Pacific—in the United States and in Southeast Asia— to ensure that both sides have a solid understanding of one another's history, culture, society, and point of view. An atmosphere of mutual respect and understanding, enhanced through regular dialogue on a broad range of issues, will go a long way toward the achievement of mutual goals and interests in the future.

REGIONAL RECOMMENDATIONS

---

1. The United States should maintain its current structure of bilateral security alliances in East Asia, and its forward deployment of military forces in the region. On balance, this American security presence contributes positively to the overall security and stability of the region, including Southeast Asia.

---

2. Recognizing that U.S.-China relations have a significant effect on the overall security situation in the Asia-Pacific region, including Southeast Asia, the United States should work with China in constructing peaceful and cooperative relations between the two countries so as to avoid the aggravation of tensions and potential conflict in the region.

---

3. Southeast Asian countries recognize that it is conducive to regional peace and prosperity to have stronger multilateral mechanisms in place for the purpose of regular consultation. In this regard, the next U.S. administration should give increased support to strengthening of regional and multilateral institutions (ARF, APEC, WTO) and approaches to deal with future economic

and security challenges in Southeast Asia, including those regional bodies that may not include the United States.

4. National sovereignty and territorial integrity are historic concerns of the countries in Southeast Asia, which have taken on increased importance given renewed ethnic and religious conflicts in the region and the recent separation of East Timor from Indonesia. In this regard, the American-led NATO military intervention in Kosovo, which seemed to emphasize the value of human rights at the expense of respect for state sovereignty and was carried out outside the framework of the United Nations, raised concerns in Southeast Asia. **In this climate, it would do well for the new American administration to reaffirm its recognition of the principles of sovereignty, territorial integrity, and national unity in Southeast Asia.**

5. **The U.S. must play a crucial role in Southeast Asia's economic recovery and growth following the Asian economic crisis, and can be helpful in supporting needed policy reforms.** It is hoped that the new U.S. administration will support the reform efforts of Southeast Asian countries by providing assistance through bilateral and multilateral channels for technical training, research, workshops, and regional meetings to strengthen the performance of government policy and regulatory initiatives in Southeast Asia and to help in the adoption of best practices in such areas as bank restructuring, commercial law, and corporate governance.

6. **The new U.S. administration should pursue a fresh round of trade talks in the WTO, but should decouple trade issues from those involving human rights.** Failure to do so could endanger the success of new initiatives to promote increased regional economic cooperation. The U.S. should also demonstrate more patience with the newer members of ASEAN as they take steps to develop more market-based economies. The willingness on the part of the U.S. to share information technology, environmental technology, and agricultural technology will help ASEAN countries to become more competitive, with benefits for both Southeast Asia and the United States in the long run.

7. **The values of democracy and human rights are widely accepted by Southeast Asians. However, the U.S. should pursue a more subtle approach in promoting democracy and human rights in Southeast Asia, one that refrains from public criticism, takes a longer-term view, and is appreciative that each country will determine its own developmental path on the basis of its own needs and its own history, culture, and circumstances.** American support to Southeast Asian countries for efforts to develop the rule of law, strengthen civil society, or implement good governance reforms are very much welcome as long as such support is requested by Southeast Asian institutions and handled with mutual respect and sensitivity.

8. There is strong concern in Southeast Asia about the decline of U.S. foreign assistance. In earlier decades, the region benefitted greatly from American assistance, particularly in such

areas as education and training. **The newer countries of ASEAN, in particular, face tremendous developmental and human resource challenges, and increased U.S. assistance could make a significant contribution toward future prosperity and to a more positive attitude in the region toward the United States.**

9. Given the increasing importance of nontraditional security issues in Southeast Asia and globally, the new U.S. administration can play an important role in providing support to regional efforts to combat transnational crimes and the trafficking of women and children, as well as helping to reduce the flow of narcotics and arms.

10. Compared to a quarter-century ago, fewer American policy-makers and officials have a deep understanding of Southeast Asia and its changing dynamics. **To reverse this trend, the new U.S. administration and Congress should devote more attention to Southeast Asian issues in an effort to develop the United States' mutual interests with Southeast Asia in a more comprehensive and consistent manner. Attention should also be paid to reversing the decline of Southeast Asian studies in American colleges and universities, in order to develop American expertise and understanding of Southeast Asia for the future.**

SOUTH ASIA

OVERVIEW

The predominant view across South Asia today is that increased
U.S. engagement in South Asia is not only welcome, but vital
for the prosperity of South Asia and its people. In this regard,
President Clinton's visit to India, Pakistan, and Bangladesh in
March 2000 was warmly received as an indication of renewed
American interest in the region. At the same time, there are
concerns in the other South Asian states that India will tend
to dominate U.S. attention in the region at the expense of the
smaller South Asian states.

While there are differing opinions regarding India's
role and intentions as the dominant player in the region, it
is the India-Pakistan conflict—exacerbated by the stalemate
in Kashmir—that is the most serious threat to regional peace
and stability. Given the intractable nature of the conflict
and America's unique role as a global super power, there is
growing sentiment in South Asia for the U.S. to play a more
active role in bringing the two sides together in dialogue
and in ensuring that cross-border tensions will be contained.
A U.S. military presence or role, however, is clearly not a
desirable development.

As important as the resolution of the India-Pakistan
conflict is to the overall security of the region, the overriding

American focus on the nuclear arms issue and the India-Pakistani rivalry runs the risk of neglecting other elements of security that may actually be of more critical importance to the region in both the short and long term. Although subnational in their origins, these other security challenges often spill across borders, threatening stability and hindering growth and progress in the region as a whole. For example, environmental security issues related to scarcity of land, water, and food supply generate substantial concern in South Asia, as does the escalation of violence and terrorism along ethnic and religious lines. The extensive trafficking of narcotics and small arms, often associated with ethnic and religious conflicts, further destabilizes efforts in the region to achieve peace and stability. Violence against women and the trafficking of women and children are additional factors inhibiting cooperation and progress.

Compared to other parts of Asia, the American propensity to emphasize democracy and human rights as key elements in its foreign policy has not caused serious problems for U.S. relations with South Asian countries. The strong democratic traditions in South Asia set it apart from other regions and provide for a common political vocabulary with the United States that should help to facilitate U.S.-South Asian dialogue and cooperation. In practice, however, the complex and changing processes of political and societal development in South Asia make it extremely difficult to build and sustain a deep sense of democratic partnership between the two sides. With regard to Pakistan, for example, many South Asians share the American concern about the current military government, in part because of their own experience with military rule or fear of a similar occurrence in their country. Indeed, many in South Asia would welcome a U.S. policy that pressed the government in Pakistan on a timeframe for an early return to civilian rule. At the same time, South Asians are conscious that too much U.S. pressure on the government in Pakistan would be counter-productive and may seriously affect the country's political and economic stability. By the same token, South Asians may be more receptive than others to American assistance in the governance field, but the focus should be more on good governance and civil society strengthening than on democracy per se.

It is the economic arena that holds the greatest potential for improved U.S. relations with South Asia. The region is increasingly supportive of economic liberalization and trade, and during the 1990s, the U.S. became the first- or second-largest foreign investor in every South Asian nation. There are considerable opportunities for U.S. companies in the areas of information technology, oil and gas exploration, infra-structure development, and textiles. In this regard, South Asian communities in the United States can play an important, constructive role in building economic and cultural links between South Asia and the United States. Certainly, con-tinued economic growth is critical if the region is to effectively address the significant political and social cleavages and widespread poverty that currently prevent the region from achieving its full potential.

On the whole, South Asians believe that their countries' relations with the United States can be an important element in promoting economic growth and positive social change throughout the region. In that context, beyond the intractable conflict and nuclear threat in India-Pakistani relations, South

Asia asks for a more comprehensive, long-term U.S. policy
toward the region that builds on current momentum toward
increased cooperation and contributes more robustly to future
stability and prosperity in the region.

SECURITY ISSUES

For the United States, the security environment in South Asia
is dominated by concerns over nuclear proliferation and, thus,
by the India-Pakistan conflict. Over the past 50 years, India
and Pakistan have fought three major wars, and nuclear tests
in 1998 by both Pakistan and India and the ongoing conflict
over Kashmir have heightened the nuclear dangers in the
region. Clearly, there is a need for India and Pakistan to find
a mutually acceptable solution on Kashmir if South Asia is
to avoid another large-scale military confrontation, one that
could involve nuclear weapons. In this regard, the United
States should actively encourage and support diplomatic efforts
to reduce tensions in the region, including respect for the line
of control, the cessation of armed cross-border incursions, and
the resumption of India-Pakistan bilateral dialogue. At the
same time, the U.S. should resist any suggestion on the part
of either country that the acquisition of nuclear capability
has strengthened its bargaining position. The region does
not wish to see U.S. military involvement in the region, and
would regard negatively any possible U.S. military intervention
for humanitarian purposes, as in Kosovo. However, increased
American diplomatic involvement, especially in conjunction
with the United Nations, would be welcomed. Such a process
could be assisted significantly by an American decision to

sign the Comprehensive Test Ban Treaty, which would serve to validate America's leadership position on nuclear security issues. Such an act by the United States would be an important

> *There is no doubt but that the dangers to stability posed by nuclear proliferation in South Asia are immense. At the same time, South Asians caution that the United States should not overlook the region's numerous other security challenges, which tend to be subnational in nature and which may well be even more critical to long-term regional stability and growth.*

confidence-building measure not only in South Asia, but throughout the world.

There is no doubt but that the dangers to stability posed by nuclear proliferation in South Asia are immense. At the same time, South Asians caution that the United States should not overlook the region's numerous other security challenges, which tend to be subnational in nature and which may well be even more critical to long-term regional stability and growth. Nontraditional security concerns are particularly relevant to South Asia: environmental security relating to food, water, and land; violence and terrorism along ethnic and religious lines; and the trafficking of narcotics and small arms. These subnational security challenges both reflect and exacerbate the complexity and fragility of states in the region, and, indeed, if left unchecked, could call into question the very nature of the sovereign state. They are also exacerbated by the misplaced priorities of government: increased military spending may help deal with immediate security challenges, but it also prevents countries in the region from devoting resources to such critical long-term challenges as education, health, human rights, and political reconciliation with alienated minority populations, all of which ultimately have repercussions in the security realm as well.

Security in South Asia, therefore, cannot be separated from its core economic and political roots. Environmental security concerns relating to water, food, and land are directly affecting many South Asians. The region suffers from a lack of fresh water due to floods, drought, and contamination of wells (as in the case of Bangladesh). Land is scarce due to soil degradation and overuse, and excessive population growth contributes to the resulting food shortage. In this context, there is substantial internal displacement of people as well as illegal migration across borders.

Violence and terrorism along ethnic and religious lines represents another subnational security challenge faced by millions of South Asians. In a region of states with extremely heterogenous populations, majority rule—even practiced under democratic norms—has strong potential to generate a sense of alienation and disenfranchisement from the mainstream political process among minority groups, as has been the case in Sri Lanka, Kashmir, Nepal, and parts of India and Pakistan. In these situations, the security forces are often manned by members of the majority community disproportionately to its representation in the country's population. Consequently, the concept of national security can become predisposed toward the task of organizing and sustaining the dominance of the majority, or can at least be seen as such by disgruntled minorities and their politically ambitious leaders.

This pattern of majority rule without full protection of minority rights often induces or exacerbates terrorism, carried out by forces within a state that are alienated and isolated and whose actions can have serious transnational consequences. In Sri Lanka and Kashmir, for example, militant groups have developed linkages with similar groups elsewhere and have turned to drug and arms trafficking to support their movements. Pakistan's opium production has tripled in the past 15 years, and it now ranks as the fourth-leading heroin producer in the world. Illicit drug production and trafficking in turn accelerates the flow of small arms, adding to the degree of criminalization and violence within society.

In sum, attention to traditional security concerns focusing exclusively at the state level cannot adequately address South Asia's complex political and social dynamics, which often have their origins at the subnational level but whose ultimate reverberations can have regional and even global consequences. The complex security environment described above requires that the United States, as the world's only superpower, begin to formulate a policy toward the region that is more comprehensive and that moves beyond the narrow focus on the security balance between India and Pakistan.

Indeed, the crucial linkage between regional security and subnational instability is dramatically illustrated by the case of

Pakistan itself. In blunt terms, there is widespread concern in the region that Pakistan, a nuclear power, is close to being a "failed state," on the verge of economic collapse. If the situation deteriorates further, the resulting political instability could ultimately lead to the disintegration of the state, or allow Islamic fundamentalism to become much more pronounced, with potentially devastating consequences for Pakistan, the region, and the world. Given the complexity of the current situation, and the severity of the potential risks involved, the

> *As the United States continues to improve and expand its bilateral relations with India, it needs to be mindful of traditional concerns about Indian domination on the part of the smaller countries of the region.*

United States should demonstrate greater patience with the current military government in Islamabad and work with the World Bank, the International Monetary Fund, and the international community to help Pakistan get back on its feet.

Finally, as the United States continues to improve and expand its bilateral relations with India, it needs to be mindful of traditional concerns about Indian domination on the part of the smaller countries of the region. South Asia is dominated by India's size, military power, and economic might, and this power asymmetry is a source of insecurity among all of India's neighbors. Moreover, the region's smaller states feel strongly that their accomplishments and their specific concerns and challenges may not be adequately appreciated by the United States because of its preoccupation with the nuclear issue and the India-Pakistani rivalry. Sri Lanka, for example, has undertaken ambitious economic reform measures but has received little notice or support from the United States. In this climate, the development of a new "U.S.-India axis," given new impetus by the end of the Cold War, expanding economic ties, and the two countries' shared concerns about China, would be a cause of concern not only in Pakistan (and China), but in the rest of South Asia as well.

ECONOMIC ISSUES

In contrast to uncertainties in the security realm, there is a strong consensus in the region that U.S.-South Asia economic relations, and U.S.-India relations in particular, are beginning to blossom and are critical to future progress in the region. There is a complementarity of interests: the U.S. is capital-abundant while South Asia is capital-scarce, and competitive labor costs in South Asia should make it an attractive base for export-oriented manufacturing. After decades of limited American economic engagement with South Asia, the United States has now become the most important trading partner and source of foreign investment for every country in South Asia except Nepal, where it ranks second to India. American investment in India totaled $1.8 billion four years ago, and that figure is now estimated at $10 billion. With the discovery of large deposits of natural gas in Bangladesh, investment from the United States has increased from $20 million in 1995 to $750 million in 1999.

The investment and trade climate has benefitted from a general movement in the region toward trade liberalization. India, for example, has slashed its average import tariff rate from 87 percent in 1991 to 21 percent in 1997. Pakistan's tariffs have also been lowered from 225 percent to 65 percent, even though such tariffs remain comparatively high. Sri Lanka's tariff rates are the most impressive, with an average import tariff level of 10 percent that could soon rival those of Southeast Asian nations. Industries particularly profiting from trade liberalization include textiles, autos, liquor, agriculture, computer hardware and accessories, and retail.

It is India, with its huge domestic market and advances in critical industries such as software, that will command most of the U.S. attention. The opening up of the insurance and financial sectors has also generated a great deal of commercial interest, while India's substantial infrastructure needs in terms of new highways, roads, bridges, ports, and energy offer significant opportunities for U.S. businesses. These same economic opportunities apply to other South Asian countries as well, to varying degrees.

The most explosive growth in India is of course in the information technology sector, where the country's software industry has shown dramatically that trade based on comparative advantage can lead to booming exports. Current software exports total slightly under $4 billion, but the U.S. National Association of Software and Services Company projects that number to increase to $50 billion by 2008. General Electric

is setting up its largest foreign research and development
facility in Bangalore, while Microsoft, Adobe, Hughes, and
Oracle are performing high-skill tasks in India. India has
given qualified support to the U.S. position on the Information
Technology Agreement, and the United States and India have
voiced the political commitment to refrain from imposing
taxes on e-commerce.

Beyond India, many South Asians also speak of the vast
potential of information technology to contribute to the economic and social betterment of the region as a whole. There
is significant potential for distance education services, for
example. The South Asian expatriate community in the United
States can play a pivotal role facilitating U.S.-South Asian
cooperation in information technology and other fields, and in
encouraging second-generation economic reforms in the region.

This generally positive outlook associated with South
Asia's progress in economic liberalization is tempered by some
continuing differences in trade policy. Points of divergence
exist on issues such as textiles, labor, and the environment.
Many South Asians perceive a sense of U.S. duplicity on trade,
as the Commerce Department promotes free trade while the
United States Trade Representative (USTR) tends to adopt
a more mercantilist approach. Most glaring is the perception
in South Asia that the Multifibre Agreement is "one of the
most blatant double standards in international trade," with
the United States being even more restrictive towards garment
exports than the European Union. While these restrictions have
hurt Indian textile exports to the United States, Bangladesh
is far more affected. Sri Lanka is also disappointed by the
level of protection accorded the United States textile sector.

In response, some in South Asia have suggested that India should retaliate with lax enforcement of its intellectual property commitments if the United States and the European Union do

On the whole, South Asians believe that the U.S. emphasis on labor and environmental standards in trade negotiations is motivated as much by the desire to protect American business interests as by a genuine concern for the well-being of workers and the environment.

not make concessions in the textile field. On the whole, South Asians believe that the U.S. emphasis on labor and environmental standards in trade negotiations is motivated as much by the desire to protect American business interests as by a genuine concern for the well-being of workers and the environment. To the extent that the United States insists on applying pressure with regard to labor, environment, and human rights concerns, South Asians do not wish to see these issues linked to the World Trade Organization.

Despite the important success of key sectors of the Indian economy, the United States should not forget that large portions of India and South Asia in general remain mired in severe poverty. Nor is the market widely accepted as a panacea for all of the region's difficulties. There is still a strong sense in South Asia that the state can and must continue to play an important role in the economy, particularly in terms of meeting basic human needs and providing the essential economic infrastructure, including health and education, that is vital for human development and ultimate prosperity. In this same vein, there is also a need for higher levels of multilateral and bilateral foreign assistance to South Asia, including from the United States, to help in the eradication of poverty and the creation of new opportunities for those currently trapped below the poverty line.

At the regional level, the countries of South Asia have been hampered in their ability to promote cross-border trade and investment in the region by the absence of effective institutional mechanisms to foster such cooperation. Despite efforts to encourage greater regional cooperation through the South Asian Association for Regional Cooperation (SAARC), the region has lagged far behind Southeast Asia in building an architecture of regional economic cooperation that would contribute to economic growth in South Asia. This same lack of regional cohesion makes it difficult for the countries of South Asia to speak with one voice in international fora or in their dealings with the United States and other actors. Two of the biggest constraints to establishing such regional cooperation are India's own traditional preference for bilateralism and the deep suspicion and distrust of Indian hegemony among the smaller states in the region, where politicians are often under pressure to be "anti-India" in their rhetoric and actions in order to maintain their popularity. Bangladesh and Nepal have excess energy supplies that could be imported by India, for example, but strong anti-India sentiment among the populations of these countries has been exploited by political leaders for their own ends, effectively putting the issue on the back burner. To overcome this problem over time, India has a critical role to play in supporting the economic growth of the region as a whole, and, in the process, allaying other state's fears and concerns about India's intentions.

POLITICAL AND SOCIAL ISSUES

As in other parts of the world, the end of the Cold War has underlined old tensions and generated new uncertainties. Ethnic and linguistic cleavages, dissident and separatist movements, and local rivalries have proliferated, threatening the region's fragile stability. At the same time, citizens in South Asia are expressing concern and frustration about the performance of their governments in addressing complex national challenges, raising questions about the future strength of democratic governance in the region.

On the whole, South Asians want their countries to develop stronger democratic institutions and practices, and to see civil society strengthened. Democracy itself as a political ideal, and as a preferred system of government, enjoys overwhelming popular support. However, the actual practice of democracy in the region has often failed to meet citizen expectations, hampered sometimes by extreme partisanship leading to policy gridlock and government paralysis, and other times by a triumph of majoritarianism at the expense of minority rights and interests leading to alienation and instability. As such, democracy in South Asia cannot be viewed through a simple ideological lens, and its challenges must be addressed with an understanding of the many complexities involved.

While South Asians respect the achievements of American democracy and share America's commitment to the democratic ideal, there are sometimes sensitivities with regard to the way the United States chooses to incorporate democracy into its foreign policy. For example, many Pakistanis are deeply skeptical of the U.S.' insistence on a quick return to democracy in that country, given that the United States was willing, for strategic reasons related to the Cold War, to tolerate an extreme form of military dictatorship supported by the United States from 1977 to 1988. Increasingly, South Asians argue that what the region truly needs from its political system is not merely the institutions and rules of formal democracy, but good governance predicated on principles of accountability and the rule of law and reinforced by a strong civil society. To the extent that the U.S. interest in encouraging democracy abroad can reflect these priorities, it will receive a more receptive welcome in South Asia. But it is also widely held in the region that political problems in countries like Pakistan, Bangladesh, and Sri Lanka cannot be solved without also addressing people's basic socio-economic needs. Issues like poverty, unemployment, and corruption affect tens of millions of people on a very personal, day-to-day basis, and in this climate there will always be those in South Asia who argue that jobs and opportunities are far more important than democracy per se.

In this regard, Pakistan looms large in the region as the most volatile state. Pakistanis are deeply frustrated by the extent to which their leaders, both civilian and military, have failed to lead the country to its full potential in the decades since independence. The wave of popular votes that brought Prime Minister Nawaz Sharif into power was predicated in part on his promises of growth-oriented economic policies. Instead, his government established capital controls and import restrictions which destroyed investor confidence, while accusations of corruption grew. Nuclear tests brought sanctions that made the economic situation even more difficult. Such was the political environment when the military takeover occurred on October 12, 1999.

Since coming to power, General Musharraf has taken steps to demonstrate sensitivity to U.S. and international reactions to his regime: martial law was never declared, the constitution was not abrogated, and parliament was not suspended. Pakistan's new government has also moved quickly

While many South Asians would welcome a return to civilian rule in Pakistan, an American insistence on Pakistan's immediate return to democracy would be generally viewed in the region as unrealistic and counterproductive.

to announce plans for devolution and possible elections. Nevertheless, in four key areas Pakistan remains in crisis: a deep economic recession, a serious foreign exchange problem, a difficult regional and security context, and a lack of visible support from the international community. Many South Asians believe that in the absence of an economic turnaround in the next six months, Pakistan will face the prospect of anarchy, a further rise in Islamic fundamentalism, and the political Balkanization of the country that will have worrisome consequences not only for Pakistan, but also for the region and the world. In this regard, while many South Asians would welcome a return to civilian rule in Pakistan, an American insistence on Pakistan's immediate return to democracy would be generally viewed in the region as unrealistic and counterproductive. While international pressure should be maintained on Pakistan to ensure that the government will be held accountable for its actions and that the next elections are free and fair, the United States should work with the IMF and the World Bank to prevent the country's economic collapse.

Another major political issue in South Asia with implications for U.S. policy is the fragmentation of politics along the lines of caste, class, and ethnicity. Generational change in the region has brought many younger, more militant individuals to the fore whose political vision tends to be dominated by their primordial loyalties, raising the specter of rising extremism in politics.

At the same time, as the world economy is changing rapidly and globalization brings increasing interaction between peoples and cultures, there is new pressure on all countries to improve their performance and their competitiveness. In this context, many South Asians are concerned about what appears to be a widening between the region's growing economic sophistication and the quality of its political leadership, including the capacity to deal with the crucial developmental challenges that will determine the region's future. At present, health and education expenditures per capita in South Asia are among the lowest in the developing world, and the region remains home to 40 percent of the world's poor, some half a billion people. Widespread poverty linked to low educational development, which in turn is linked to the low status of women, poses an ever greater handicap in the face of increasing economic integration and competition. If left unchecked, the widening gulf between private and public schools, English-speaking and non-English speaking citizens, and between the urban well-off and the rural poor could lead to further political difficulties down the line as large portions of South Asia remain cut off from full participation in the region's opportunities and successes.

In short, the challenges facing political ability and sustainable democracy in South Asia are ultimately inseparable from the challenges of ensuring continued economic growth and maintaining social cohesion in the countries of the region. Greater appreciation of these linkages on the part of the United States would go a long way toward improving further the generally more positive atmosphere in U.S.-South Asia relations that has been developing in recent years. Improvements in state-to-state relations can also be enhanced by more extensive people-to-people contacts, drawing on a shared commitment to democratic values and assisted by the growing number of South Asians with personal and family ties to the United States. Greater familiarity, whether through private sector interactions, academic programs, or citizen exchanges, will help to alleviate the distrust and misunderstanding of earlier years and provide a strong foundation for what could be a much more promising future in U.S.-South Asian relations.

REGIONAL RECOMMENDATIONS

1. The United States should pursue a more vigorous role in easing India-Pakistan tensions, but should be careful to limit that role to a diplomatic one.

There is broad-based acknowledgment, in South Asia and abroad, that stability in the region cannot be achieved without successful resolution of the India-Pakistan dispute over Kashmir. Despite this, no obvious solution to this longstanding disagreement is apparent to the disputing parties or to would-be mediators of the crisis. Drawing on its history of alliance with Pakistan and the recent strides made in U.S.-Indian relations, the United States should seek a more active role in encouraging the two nations to reduce cross-border tensions and to find a long-term solution to this dispute. It can best do so by playing the role of balancer, by helping to ensure that existing lines of command and control are respected as well as by urging the two sides to increase dialogue on Kashmir and on the issues that radiate from this conflict. In doing so, however, the United States must make clear that its role is strictly a diplomatic one and that the United States will not play a direct role in providing security in this situation, for either or both sides. Moreover, the United States should resist any suggestion by either India or Pakistan that their acquisition of nuclear weapons has strengthened their bargaining position vis-à-vis the other.

---

2. The United States should sign and ratify the Comprehensive Test Ban Treaty (CTBT).

The ability of the United States to advocate and promote nuclear nonproliferation, in South Asia and elsewhere in the world, would be strengthened by its accession to the CTBT. Although ratification is likely to be a lengthy and protracted process, the United States should sign the Treaty at the earliest opportunity, to underscore its commitment to nuclear nonproliferation and to encourage other countries to move toward compliance with nonproliferation regimes.

---

3. The United States should give greater attention in its South Asia policy to nontraditional security threats which can exacerbate internal and cross-border tensions.

Although the threat of a nuclear exchange between India and Pakistan cannot be taken lightly, U.S. policy is in danger of taking a myopic approach to South Asian security by focusing solely on this issue. Transnational and subnational threats in the region—including environmental security (of food, water, and land), ethnic and religious violence, narcotics trafficking, and small arms flows—can ignite new domestic and cross-border conflicts or worsen existing ones. To help avert crises in this dimension, U.S. policymakers must view security in South Asia in a social as well as a strategic dimension, and craft new policies to respond to these new threats.

---

4. The United States should shore up its relations with the smaller states of South Asia as it broadens and deepens its relations with India.

As the United States and India solidify and advance relations, in line with the recent Summit, the U.S. must also make a deliberate attempt to strengthen its ties with the smaller states of South Asia. Doing so will avoid reinforcing the political and economic asymmetry in the region, with India at the center, which has made it difficult for South Asia to develop effective regional frameworks for cooperation, including SAARC. Moreover, a balanced policy will position the United States to encourage greater regional cooperation, which in turn will help boost economies in the region and contribute to the reduction of tensions in South Asia.

---

5. The United States should increase its development assistance to South Asia to alleviate poverty, and should channel more of that assistance through bilateral instruments.

Although South Asian middle classes are emerging, twice the number of people in the region—approximately 800 million—live in severe poverty. Even in countries that are becoming

technological players, such as India, the gap between the upper
and middle classes and the poor is more serious than in other
regions. It is imperative that U.S. policy recognize and help
alleviate this imbalance, for security as well as humanitarian
reasons. Increased flows of development assistance could, for
example, have a significant and positive impact in strengthening social safety nets, which could help alleviate internal as
well as cross-border tensions. Although American foreign aid
continues to decline in real terms, U.S. policymakers should
not allow a penny-wise pound-foolish approach to prevail.
Beyond increasing levels, policymakers should endeavor to
channel a greater proportion of assistance through bilateral
rather than multilateral instruments. This will have a
two-pronged benefit: enabling the United States to apply
assistance more directly to South Asian needs it has identified,
in discussion with both governments and civil society groups,
and helping to solidify U.S. bilateral relations in the region.

6. While supporting democratic trends in South Asia, the United
   States should focus more on function—emphasizing good
   governance and transparency—than on form.

In contrast to East and Southeast Asia, in which significant
portions of the population still live under authoritarian rule,
South Asia has demonstrated brisk, if not unbroken, progress in
democratic development in the past decade. The United States
should continue to support this positive trend, but it should
reconfigure its democracy promotion policy to reflect new concerns. First, rather than continuing to emphasize democratic

forms of government categorically, the United States should assist South Asian countries in developing more efficient and accountable government. This instrumental, rather than ideological, approach will help prevent democratic backsliding and reversals, because it addresses the fundamental need for government to formulate policies and provide services that improve the lives of citizens. Such an emphasis also helps prevent the disillusionment with elected government which spurred the present political situation in Pakistan. Second, a greater proportion of U.S. assistance should be directed toward South Asian civil society groups. This will have a two-pronged benefit: improving the delivery of social services while strengthening the democratic fabric of South Asian nations.

SUMMARY RECOMMENDATIONS FOR U.S. POLICY IN ASIA

---

1. In formulating and implementing key areas of its Asia policy, the United States should utilize bilateral consultations more extensively and, where possible, take a multilateral approach.

Although there is widespread recognition of the leadership role played by the United States in both Asian security and economics, there is also increasing ambivalence—even among America's Asian allies—about the way in which the United States conducts its role as the primary power. In issues of vital national security and, to some extent, of trade, nations invariably make bottom-line decisions based on their own national interests. However, the nations of Asia and the United States have a common interest in regional stability and the reduction of tensions, as well as in promoting trade which promotes economic well-being. As a guarantor of Asian security and a major economic force, it does not ultimately benefit the United States to take a unilateral approach to such issues.

U.S. policymakers must therefore make more deliberate and extensive efforts to consult Asian leaders on key security issues while they are in the process of formulating security policies. The most important example in this regard is the need for greater consultations on the development of an American national missile defense system, as well as a possible theater missile defense. Where multilateral consultations are possible, such as on the Korean peninsula, the United States should support and advance such a framework. These multilateral arrangements are likely to be *ad hoc* for the foreseeable future, but may carry with them the seeds of a future regional security architecture. In the dimension of trade, more frequent consultations between the United States and its trading partners will help establish a regular process of dialogue that may avert or reduce conflicts. This is particularly important as Asian nations continue to recover from the 1997-1998 financial crisis, and as the United States faces a possible slowdown in its own economy.

Where possible, consultations should be expanded and formalized in broad-based dialogues with Asian countries on a range of issues to promote ongoing discussion of a long-term "Pacific Vision." Modeled after the U.S.-Japan Common Agenda, these dialogues should identify issues of common interest and concern beyond the parameters of traditional policy. These issue areas might include the environment, human rights, care of aging populations, and the gap between the "haves" and "have-nots." Dialogues should be based in societal as well as governmental relations, and include representatives from executive branches, legislatures, media, business sectors, nongovernmental organizations, and academia. These networks will enable Northeast Asians and Americans to identify shared interests, explore differences of opinion in a constructive manner, and improve each side's understanding of the other's political and social dynamics.

2. The United States should acknowledge and support regional institution-building efforts across Asia. It should encourage even those regional proposals that exclude a formal role for the U.S., but that support shared goals of reducing tensions, promoting free trade, and adhering to the rule of law.

In the wake of the Asian financial crisis, the need to examine and to strengthen regional frameworks has become more starkly apparent. At the present time, the main focus of these efforts is on financial architecture, at the global, regional, and subregional level. As countries recover from the crisis and as China approaches entry into the World Trade Organization, interest is growing in adherence to common trade regulations and multilateral regimes. At the same time, the short-term cost of such change to countries whose systems and practices do not yet conform to the requirements of the advanced economies is equally apparent. Protectionism, different rates of economic growth and reform among trade partners, and legal systems that are ill-equipped to enforce global trade rules must be addressed and remedied. This is complicated by some resentments over the role of the United States and the international financial institutions during the financial crisis. As a result of these factors, new regional and subregional groups and arrangements are under consideration in Asia, some of which exclude the United States and other Western economic powers.

The United States should take a four-pronged approach to these developments. First, it should continue to press Asian governments for financial and economic reforms which will benefit the cause of regional free trade, as well as individual countries. Second, the United States should employ and demonstrate patience and a more long-term approach with Asian trading partners where there is a good-faith effort to remove barriers to free trade. Third, where possible, the United States should work toward multilateral financial regimes, even if it means scaling back bilateral trade efforts and forfeiting some of the short-term gains to be had from bilateral pressure. Lastly, the United States should acknowledge and support regional and subregional groupings which advance the cause of free trade in Asia, whether or not they offer a formal role for the United States.

In comparison to trade, regional security architecture in Asia is a less certain and more distant goal. However, the United States should support an expansion of security dialogues (and discussion of future frameworks) wherever possible, as well as promote *ad hoc* arrangements, such as the Four Party Talks on Korea, to address regional security concerns. In doing so, the U.S. should not take or encourage a parochial approach, by ignoring the spillover effects of potential conflicts in the region. A serious and prolonged con-frontation in the Taiwan Straits, for example, will inevitably affect the security environment not only of Northeast Asia, but also of Southeast Asia.

Lastly, where possible the United States should encour-age attempts in South Asia to build regional consensus on a range of issues, and ultimately a regional framework, by lending its support to the South Asian Association for Regional Cooperation (SAARC).

---

3. The United States should downplay pressure for Asian countries to build Western-style democracies and emphasize the need for governments to be more responsive and accountable.

The demand for good governance is growing in many Asian countries that are still under some form of authoritarian rule, as well as those that are presently democratizing. Abandoning a high-profile democracy promotion effort in favor of encouraging more transparent and accountable government will enable the United States to promote greater openness in a range of Asian states, rather than only in those that have made a formal commitment to democracy. This instrumental, rather than ideological approach, also helps prevent backsliding and reversals in new democracies, because it addresses the fundamental need for government to formulate policies and provide services that improve the lives of citizens. Moreover, this approach is more appropriate for an outside actor (and more acceptable to most Asians), since it does not advocate or prescribe an exact form of government. American support to Asian countries for efforts to develop the rule of law, strengthen civil society, or implement good governance reforms are generally welcome as long as such support is requested by Asian institutions and handled with mutual respect and sensitivity.

4. The United States should recognize the rise and development of civil society organizations in a range of Asian countries, and strengthen linkages between American civil society organizations and their Asian counterparts.

Just as policymaking in the United States has become more open to citizens' concerns, so is Asian governance and policy-making becoming more pluralistic. During the Cold War, American policymakers needed only to interact with their counterparts in Asian governments. In order to understand Asian concerns and craft more effective policies, U.S. policy-makers must now take into account the views of a broader spectrum of Asian actors. Beyond official policymaking, U.S.-Asian relations will benefit from increased contact between Asian nongovernmental organizations and their American counterparts, particularly on issues of common concern (public health, education, environmental pollution). These linkages can be nurtured in a number of ways, ranging from assistance for programs that link NGOs across the Pacific, to the addition of an NGO dimension to official dialogues.

5. American universities should be encouraged to strengthen Asian studies programs, to provide a broader base of educators in Asian affairs.

Increasing and maintaining American interest in Asian affairs, which is crucial to formulating policies that effectively promote U.S. interests in Asia, must go beyond dialogues and be rooted in the American education system. Programs in Asian studies should be strengthened, and more Americans should be encouraged to study in Asia. There is currently a serious imbalance in this regard. For example, presently only 1,400 American students attend Japanese educational institutions, while 40,000 Japanese students are enrolled in American colleges and universities. Long-term beneficial relations between the United States and the countries of Asia will depend on the existence of communities of policymakers, scholars, and everyday citizens who are knowledgeable about the history, culture, structures, and views of their partners across the Pacific.

6. The United States should maintain its current structure of bilateral security alliances and agreements in the Asia-Pacific region, and its forward deployment of military forces in the region.

In the future, minor adjustments to this structure may be required in light of security and political developments in the region. On balance, however, the American security presence contributes positively to the overall security and stability of both the Northeast and Southeast Asia regions.

7. The new U.S. administration should join with Asian nations in pursuing a fresh round of trade talks in the World Trade Organization.

The lead-up to such a round should be pursued through bilateral trade dialogues as well as through such institutions as APEC. In the pursuit of a more free trade environment with its Asian partners, the U.S. should apply conditionality sparingly if at all.

---

8. The United States should increase its development assistance to Asia, where needed, to alleviate poverty and address basic human needs.

In Southeast Asia and South Asia in particular, levels of economic development, and severe discrepancies in economic levels within countries, persist. In Southeast Asia, the newer members of ASEAN face tremendous economic and human resource challenges. In South Asia, although middle classes are strengthening, twice the number of people—approximately 800 million—live in severe poverty. U.S. policy should do more to recognize and alleviate these problems, for security as well as humanitarian reasons. Increased flows of development assistance can, for example, have a significant and positive impact on strengthening social safety nets, which in turn can help alleviate internal as well as cross-border tensions.

Although American foreign aid continues to decline in real terms, U.S. policymakers should not allow a penny-wise pound-foolish approach to prevail. Increased American assistance will not only make a much-needed contribution to meeting basic human needs and laying a strong groundwork for future development through human and institutional capacity-building; it will also serve to generate goodwill in the region and encourage cooperative relations between the United States and the countries of Asia.

9. The United States should give greater attention in its Asia policy to nontraditional security threats which can exacerbate internal and cross-border tensions.

Although threats in the conventional security arena in Asia, ranging from tensions in the Taiwan Straits to the India-Pakistan dispute over Kashmir, largely define U.S. security and diplomatic policy in Asia, the United States is in danger of taking a myopic approach. Transnational and subnational threats in the region—including environmental security (of food, water, and land), ethnic and religious tensions, narcotics trafficking, and small arms flows—can ignite new domestic and cross-border conflicts or worsen existing ones. To help avert crises in this dimension, U.S. policymakers must view security in Asia in a social as well as a strategic dimension, and craft new policies to respond to these new threats. Where possible, the United States should support regional efforts to combat these problems, which will have the dual effect of reducing threats and strengthening regional infrastructure.

10. The United States should sign and ratify the Comprehensive Test Ban Treaty.

The ability of the United States to advocate and promote nuclear nonproliferation, in Asia and throughout the world, would be strengthened by its accession to the Comprehensive Test Ban Treaty. Although ratification is likely to be a lengthy and protracted process, the United States should sign the Treaty at the earliest opportunity, to underscore its commitment to nuclear nonproliferation and to encourage other countries to move toward compliance with nonproliferation regimes.

ASIAN REGIONAL WORKSHOP PARTICIPANTS

NORTHEAST ASIA REGIONAL WORKSHOP: TOKYO, JAPAN

CHAIR:
Mr. Tadashi Yamamoto
President
Japan Center for International Exchange
Tokyo, Japan

The Honorable Sanjaasuregin Oyun
Member of the State Great Hural
Ulaanbaatar, Mongolia

Ms. Cheung Man-yee
Principal Representative
The Government of the Hong Kong SAR
Tokyo, Japan

Dr. Yoshio Murakami
General Director, International Affairs
The Asahi Shimbun
Tokyo, Japan

Dr. Cheng-Yi Lin
Research Fellow
Institute of European and American Studies, Academia Sinica
Taipei, Taiwan

Dr. Vladimir I. Ivanov
Research Division Senior Researcher
Economic Research Institute for Northeast Asia
Niigata, Japan

Mr. Wu Baiyi
Deputy Director, Division of Research
China Foundation for International and Strategic Studies
Beijing, China

Dr. Byung-Joon Ahn
Professor of Political Science
Yonsei University
Seoul, Korea

Mr. Puntsag Tsagaan
Vice President
Premier International, Inc.
Ulaanbaatar, Mongolia

The Honrable Hiroaki Fujii
President
The Japan Foundation
Tokyo, Japan

Dr. In-taek Hyun
Associate Professor, Department of Political Science
Korea University
Seoul, Korea

Dr. Yoshihide Soeya
Professor of International Relations
Faculty of Law, Keio University
Tokyo, Japan

Dr. Wang Jisi
Director
Institute of American Studies
Chinese Academy of Social Sciences
Beijing, China

SOUTHEAST ASIA REGIONAL WORKSHOP: BANGKOK, THAILAND

CHAIR:
Dr. Pranee Thiparat
Director, Institute for Security and International Studies
Chulalongkorn University
Bangkok, Thailand

Mr. Nguyen Manh Hung
Director, Americas Department
Ministry of Foreign Affairs
Hanoi, Vietnam

Dr. Suzaina Kadir
Assistant Professor, Department of Political Science
National University of Singapore
Singapore

Professor Dato' Dr. Zakaria Hj. Ahmad
Dean, Faculty of Social Sciences and Humanities
Universiti Kebangsaan Malaysia
Kuala Lumpur, Malaysia

Professor Gordon de Brouwer
Australia-Japan Research Center
Asia Pacific School of Economics and Management
The Australian National University
Canberra, Australia

Professor Peter Drysdale
Executive Director
Asia Pacific School of Economics and Management
The Australian National University
Canberra, Australia

Mr. Anucha Chansuriya
Executive, The Charoen Pokphand Group, Co., Ltd.
Bangkok, Thailand

Dr. Melina Nathan
Associate Research Fellow, Nanyang Technological University
Institute of Defence and Strategic Studies
Singapore

Mr. Kavi Chongkittavorn
Executive Editor
The Nation Multimedia Group
Bangkok, Thailand

Ambassador Done Somvorachit
Director General, Department of Europe and Americas
Ministry of Foreign Affairs
Vientiane, Lao PDR

Mr. Sommay Phothisane
Director, Research Division
Ministry of Foreign Affairs
Vientiane, Lao PDR

Dr. Kao Kim Hourn
Executive Director
Cambodian Institute for Cooperation and Peace
Phnom Penh, Cambodia

Dr. Than Sina
First Vice Governor
City of Phnom Penh
Phnom Penh, Cambodia

Dr. Rizal Sukma
Director of Studies
Centre for Strategic and International Studies
Jakarta, Indonesia

Mr. Dino Patti Djalal
Counsellor
Directorate of International Organizations
Ministry of Foreign Affairs
Jakarta, Indonesia

Dr. Khadija Md. Khalid
Lecturer
Faculty of Economics and Administration
University of Malaya
Kuala Lumpur, Malaysia

Dr. Jesus Estanislao
President
Foundation for Community Building in the Asia-Pacific, Inc.
Manila, Philippines

Ms. Maria Consuelo Ortuoste
Director
Center for International Relations and Strategic Studies
Foreign Service Institute
Manila, Philippines

Ms. Amalina Murad
Diplamatic Officer
Political II Department
Ministry of Foreign Affairs
Bandar Seri Begawan, Brunei Darussalam

SOUTH ASIA REGIONAL WORKSHOP: DHAKA, BANGLADESH

CHAIR:
Mr. Abul Ahsan
Vice President
Independent University of Bangladesh
Dhaka, Bangladesh

Mr. Enayetullah Khan
Editor-in-Chief, *Holiday*
Dhaka, Bangladesh

Dr. Rahul Mukherji
Assistant Research Professor
Centre for Policy Research
New Delhi, India

Mr. Milinda Moragoda
Chairman
Mercantile Merchant Bank Ltd.
Colombo, Sri Lanka

Mr. Ken Balendra
Chairman
John Keells Holdings
Colombo, Sri Lanka

Dr. Imtiaz Ahmed
Professor of International Relations
University of Dhaka
Dhaka, Bangladesh

Mr. Kanak Dixit
Editor, *Himal Magazine*
Kathmandu, Nepal

Mr. Gopal B. Thapa
Under Secretary
General Administration Division
Ministry of Foreign Affairs
Kathmandu, Nepal

Dr. Hafiz Pasha
Managing Director
Social Policy and Development Centre
Islamabad, Pakistan

Dr. Partha Ghosh
Director
Indian Council of Social Science Research
New Delhi, India

ABOUT THE AUTHORS

TADASHI YAMAMOTO – JAPAN

Mr. Tadashi Yamamoto is President of the Japan Center for International Exchange (JCIE) which he founded in 1970. He is currently a member as well as the Japanese Director of the Trilateral Commission, the UK-Japan 21st Century Group, the Japanese-German Forum, and the Korea-Japan Forum. Mr. Yamamoto also serves as board member of the Asian Community Trust, and the Japan NPO Center. He was a member and Executive Director of the Prime Minister's Commission on Japan's Goals in the 21st Century and submitted its report in January, 2000. He is editor/author of several books on civil society and the nonprofit sector including: <u>Nonprofit Sector in Japan</u>, <u>Deciding the Public Good</u>, <u>Emerging Civil Society in the Asia Pacific Community</u>, and <u>The Corporate-NGO Partnership in Asia Pacific</u>. Mr. Yamamoto received his M.B.A. from Marquette University, U.S.A.

PRANEE THIPARAT – THAILAND

Dr. Pranee Thiparat is currently a full-time lecturer in the Department of International Relations at Chulalongkorn University and Director of the Institute for Security and International Studies (ISIS) in Bangkok. In addition, since 1998, she has served as an advisor to the House Foreign Relations Committee of the Thai National Assembly. She is also a regular guest lecturer on U.S.-related topics at the Army, Navy, Air Force, and Police Academies and the Parliamentary Training Institute. She is the co-host of a weekly, two-hour radio program on world affairs, as well as a regular commentator on other Thai media programs. She previously served as Director of the American and Canadian Studies Program, an interdisciplinary research unit under the auspices of the Vice President for Research Affairs. Dr. Pranee's most recent publications include: <u>US Congress in the 1990s: Critical Issues</u> (in Thai); <u>Collected Articles on the 1996 U.S. Presidential Election</u> (in Thai); and <u>Regional Conflict Management: The Role of ASEAN and the Spratlys Disputes</u> (in English). She received her Ph.D. in politics from Princeton University, U.S.A.

ABUL AHSAN – BANGLADESH

Ambassador Abul Ahsan is Vice President of the Independent University in Bangladesh. He is an active participant and member of the Executive Committee of the Coalition for Action on South Asian Cooperation (CASAC), which organizes workshops to discuss the prospects and problems of regional cooperation in South Asia and makes recommendations to heads of government. Previously, he was Chairman of the Bangladesh Fair Election Monitoring Alliance. Ambassador Ahsan also had a distinguished diplomatic career, serving as the Former Secretary General of the South Asian Association for Regional Cooperation and Bangladesh's Ambassador to the United States. He has written a book entitled <u>SAARC: A Perspective</u>, and regularly contributes to newspapers and magazines on political, educational, and cultural matters. Ambassador Ahsan holds a M.A. in Economics from the University of Dhaka and a M.A. in International Relations from Tufts University's Fletcher School of Law and Diplomacy, U.S.A.